THE
CULTURAL
CONNECTION

An essay on
Culture and Government Policy
in Canada

BERNARD
OSTRY

with an introduction by
Robert Fulford

McClelland and Stewart

Copyright © 1978 McClelland and Stewart Limited

All rights reserved

ISBN: Paper, 0-7710-6900-6
Case, 0-7710-6912-X

McClelland and Stewart Limited
The Canadian Publishers
25 Hollinger Road
Toronto, Ontario, M4B 3G2

Excerpts, p. 206, from "Choruses" and
"The Rock," from *Collected Poems 1909-
1962* by T. S. Eliot, reprinted by
permission of the author and Faber and
Faber Ltd., Publishers.

Printed and bound in Canada

Canadian Cataloguing in Publication Data
Ostry, Bernard, 1927 –
The cultural connection

Includes index.
ISBN 0-7710-6900-6

1. Canada – Intellectual life – Addresses, essays,
lectures. 2. Arts – Canada – Management –
Addresses, essays, lectures. 3. Art and state –
Canada – Addresses, essays, lectures. I. Title.

NX770.C2087   354′.71′0085   C78-001433-2

THE
CULTURAL
CONNECTION

To Adam and Jonathan
with love and hope

Contents

Acknowledgments

This essay could not have been written in the four months made available to me without the help of friends and colleagues and the assistance of a number of institutions. Under the Executive Development Leave Program of the Government of Canada, for whose existence I am grateful, I was able to take time off to write this essay. Thus, my first thanks are to the Prime Minister and his advisers for having granted me leave. I should add that any royalties the book may earn will be paid to the Receiver General for Canada.

I owe a special debt to the National Museums of Canada and Carleton University. Each provided me with accommodation and clerical and library assistance.

I have to thank Professor John Meisel of Queen's University and his students for the chance to develop these ideas in lectures and seminars, and for his encouragement to persevere when he asked me to turn them into an essay for his seminar at Yale. To Mr. David Silcox who made me welcome to his classes at York University I am also grateful.

Many of my friends took the trouble to read the manuscript at various stages, and gave invaluable advice. I am especially indebted to Mr. R. Gordon L. Fairweather, the Rev. David MacDonald and the Hon. Gérard Pelletier; Professors Roy Daniells, Jean-Charles Falardeau, W. L. Morton, John Porter, Brian Segal and Peter Waite; Mr. André Vachon of the Royal Society; to friends who are writers: Madeleine Gobeil, Martin Goodman, Eric Koch and Christina McCall Newman; and to personal friends and colleagues: André Bachand, André Fortier, Reeves Haggan, Tim Porteous, George and Allison Ignatieff and Jean-Noël Tremblay.

This essay would have been considerably weaker had I not been able to count upon the help of Henry Hindley, who contributed not only research but also the wisdom drawn from his extensive experience of cultural development in this country during his many years of distinguished government service.

I am happy to acknowledge the contribution of Kildare Dobbs who, ever since my return to this country twenty years ago, has helped me formulate my views on cultural matters and turn bureaucratic prose into understandable English.

I owe a debt to Mlle. Huguette Poitras for providing me with the perspective of a young Québécois on the culture of contemporary Québec. This was in addition to the advice from old friends like the Most Reverend Georges-Henri Lévesque and Senator the Hon. Maurice Lamontagne, to whom my obligation will be obvious.

Above all I must acknowledge the patient forbearance of my personal secretary, Brigitte Komocki, and of Heather Ann Howe, who was for years my special assistant at the Museums. Both of them, and others unnamed, volunteered hours of assistance, for which I am deeply grateful.

My wife Sylvia deserves more than the traditional nod, since she cheerfully put up with my troubles in writing while trying to rewrite her own labour economics textbook. I could no more do without her than our country could.

Any virtue this essay may have belongs to all these friends: its vices are my own.

Introduction

Bernard Ostry's account of government policies in culture arrives at a delicate moment. This year the state-supported cultural institutions of Canada are pausing for breath after a period of unprecedented expansion. In one generation, apparently almost by accident, Canada changed from a country in which the federal government's cultural role was severely limited to a country in which that role is pervasive. In 1958, when the Canada Council was in its early stages, Canadians still debated whether government had a proper part to play in cultural affairs. The Canada Council had been given only grudging assent by Parliament, and Canadian artists and intellectuals were still suspicious of the idea of state support for theatre, music, films and literature. In 1978, by contrast, every significant part of the Canadian artistic community receives subsidies from various governments, and all the evidence we have suggests that the public finds this acceptable.

This state aid for culture has changed in almost every particular the arts as practised in Canada. An accomplished Canadian painter, for example, now takes it for granted that many of his or her pictures will be sold to the federal government. An accomplished Canadian playwright now takes it for granted that his or her plays will be produced, professionally, in theatres that are state supported. A Canadian musician of talent looks naturally for employment by state-supported orchestras. Most important, to choose a career in the arts in the 1970s is no longer the foolish, Quixotic gesture it seemed to many of my generation in the 1950s.

These changes are now part of the structure of Canadian culture, but it is important to remember that they are relatively new. Artists and audiences under thirty-five take them for granted; those slightly older may still regard them as something of a miracle – as earth-shaking as it was (by many of us) unexpected. It is also important to understand that these developments were never planned: they came about by improvisation, sometimes inspired and sometimes clumsy.

The late 1970s are not a particularly happy period for those concerned with the economics of culture. In the early 1970s many of our institutions began to take for granted the steady – and sometimes spectacular – growth they had been experiencing for years; they began to see the federal and provincial treasuries as bottomless wells. At the same time, our universities and colleges were graduating thousands of student artists who expected to find places as professionals within the culture of the country. Both of these expectations have been frustrated by the slowdown – sometimes it seems almost a full stop – of government spending in recent years. The result is that many of our cultural institutions have entered a period of frustration, bitterness and introspection, in which the old issues surrounding government support are beginning to be debated in a fresh context.

Bernard Ostry is ideally suited by background to contribute to the enlargement of this debate. His career has ranged across several of the agencies and government departments which form the story he tells here. A professional historian, he has directed the Humanities and Social Science Research Councils, been an executive with the Canadian Broadcasting Corporation, an Assistant

Under Secretary of State, and Secretary General of the National Museums of Canada. He has served with certain of these institutions during some of their most creative as well as some of their most difficult years. He was supervisor of public affairs in Ottawa at the CBC when it endured the bitter struggle over *This Hour Has Seven Days*. He was one of the authors of *To Know and Be Known*, the federal government report on information which suggested that Canadian governments operate more openly and proposed that freedom of information be guaranteed by our constitution. He was at the Department of the Secretary of State when it launched Opportunities for Youth (OFY) which led to the creation of the Local Initiatives Program (LIP), New Horizons and Explorations, each of which brought other departments and the Canada Council into culture in fresh ways and each of which he helped establish. He headed the National Museums Corporation during the period when the Pelletier approach – "democratization and decentralization" – was put into effect through everything from large grants for associated museums to the Discovery Train. Now, as Deputy Minister in the Department of Communications, he is once more at the eye of a cultural hurricane, dealing with the pressures of overlapping federal-provincial jurisdictions as they play over yet another aspect of our national life.

Ostry makes the point that Québec in various ways has given culture (defined in its broadest sense, to include language) a large place in its public and political life – and that this is one of the many things that sets Québec apart from the other nine provinces and the federal government. But he also argues that in all of Canada, including Québec, we still possess only a rudimentary understanding of culture's place in our existence. We might go further than that and suggest that we have also hardly begun to understand our cultural institutions, such as the Canada Council and comprehend why they work or don't work.

He tries to define, for instance, the arm's-length relationship between politicians and arts bureaucrats that must exist if those bureaucrats are to maintain the respect of the arts community and function appropriately. The Canada Council established its legitimacy because from the beginning its independence from political interference was clearly established, and Ostry is right to reaffirm that independence not only for the Council but for the other agencies involved with culture. In this respect, cultural policy must differ sharply from policy as it is applied to most arms of government. Ostry's detailed examination of this crucial issue – one which may well become, in the near future, a subject of great controversy – is the first statement of its kind ever to emerge from a senior official in Ottawa. That in itself is proof that we have hardly begun to examine the revolution in our cultural life that we have lived through.

Ostry calls for a continuing public debate that will involve artists, art officials and the arts public, and he insists that only through a debate of this kind can we evolve policies that will provide rational support for the arts in an atmosphere of freedom. *The Cultural Connection* will more than justify its existence if it stimulates such a debate. It is a book that necessarily looks back over what has happened to us in the past, but it should be seen much more as a beginning than as an end. It is a map of the territory we have covered, but it hints at frontiers still unexplored.

Robert Fulford
August 1978

xiv

Where There Is No Vision,
The People Perish.

Proverbs 29:18

ONE

Culture, however we define it, is central to everything we do and think. It is what we do and the reason why we do it, what we wish and why we imagine it, what we perceive and how we express it, how we live and in what manner we approach death. It is our environment and the patterns of our adaptation to it. It is the world we have created and are still creating; it is the way we see that world and the motives that urge us to change it. It is the way we know ourselves and each other; it is our web of personal relationships, it is the images and abstractions that allow us to live together in communities and nations. It is the element in which we live.

Anything so essential and pervasive is easy to overlook. Air is also our element, and air is invisible, odourless, tasteless, transparent. Without it we die. We know a little about air and how the oxygen in it keeps us alive. But we have only just begun to notice the centrality of culture to the life of human communities and nations. We have barely arrived at the stage of a phlogiston theory preceding the discovery of oxygen – to pursue the analogy with air.

1

That is why I am attempting this essay on government and cultural policy in Canada. I am convinced that culture, to which I shall try to attach a more precise meaning later on, is the essential element in any nation and ought to be seen as such by democratic governments and the citizens who elect them. The governments of communist and many socialist republics perceive it all too well; for them it is something to be manipulated and controlled, used and orchestrated for the dominant conception of "the public good." But the absence of policy in parliamentary democracies can also lead to manipulation or orchestration. What is needed is a wise husbandry and the will to give culture freedom and room to grow without directing it. And this requires a conscious effort by governments and voters as well as by artists who, as custodians, stand in a special relationship to culture.

The business of governments is normally with what are perceived as substantial and material things, like finance, the economy, defence, communications, civil order and the administration of justice. Politicians and public alike understand the connection between these things and the protection of the physical integrity of their country. But governments and citizens also concern themselves, and need to concern themselves, with what are perceived as the insubstantial and imponderable things which are, in effect, what all the other substantial things are about, and which amount to the integrity and spirit of the nation. That these insubstantial things are real may be inferred from the fact that in Canada, over the past ten years, the federal government alone has spent about 2 per cent of its total budget on what it narrowly defines as culture – that is, currently almost a billion dollars every year – an incomplete figure that ought to be impressive even to those who do not care to be impressed.[1]

It is sometimes argued that we cannot and should

2

not think about culture in any connected way and that there is no need for a comprehensive public discussion and government policy in this area: that it is good enough to deal with culture timidly, in a piecemeal fashion.[2] This does not seem to me a responsible or rational way to view the spending of more than a billion federal dollars per year. I shall argue for a *policy*, openly arrived at by *debate*, which in the simplest terms means publicly choosing one course rather than another. A policy makes it possible to introduce reason and order into what we are already doing; publicly arrived at, it allows us to choose more rationally the possible courses, even the right course, for the Canadian confederation of the future, and to have hope it will become firmly rooted.

The question whether organized society should bother at all with culture, with questions of the mind and imagination, occurs against a background of differing perceptions of what culture is and what governments should do about it. Most Québec political leaders, for instance, have demanded for decades and still demand that all federal monies voted in this area should be turned over to their provincial treasury; they recognize the centrality of culture in the development of the sense of community essential to the preservation of a minority's identity. They equate certain conditions of life with *their* cultural security and not necessarily Canada's. But every province spends some of its revenues on culture, some linking it with education, others with recreation or leisure or sport. The division of general responsibilities between the federal and other governments under the British North America Act may be described as a natural one, in the sense that those concerns nearest to us are managed by the nearest government, although, having said that, we might argue about the meaning of "near." Which is nearer, the television set in the living room or the public

3

school down the road? However that may be, under our system of education, perhaps the most fragmented in the world,[3] it has not proved possible to impart a sense of common history and destiny or, which is just as important, a true understanding of our *un*common variety.[4] The unresolved conflict which Lord Durham perceived in the generation preceding Confederation and which he expressed so trenchantly in his famous Report remains to haunt us all: "I expected to find a contest between a government and a people: I found two nations warring in the bosom of a single state: I found a struggle, not of principles, but of races." Yet one hundred and fifty years later, we possess even fewer unifying institutions: the influence of organized religion has changed dramatically, where it has not seriously declined; even Canadian political parties of the same stripe are often split between federal and provincial viewpoints. It seems obvious that, apart from other considerations, the federal government has a clear responsibility – if we are to have a country at all – to encourage the growth of that missing sense of a common heritage and destiny. The federal task is to ensure that we "connect."

This is not to argue for what the poet and scholar Eli Mandel has denounced as a "vicious centralism."[5] A century ago, Thomas Carlyle told us what "The great law of culture is: Let each become all that he was created capable of being." I am arguing not so much for national unity as for national integrity, truth to ourselves, to each other, and to the facts of our history. Still less do I advocate a jurisdictional exclusiveness, federal or provincial propaganda, or any sort of manipulation of Canadian artists or cultural institutions. I am thinking of a policy of cultural development in the sense in which my colleagues on the International Fund for the Promotion of Culture of UNESCO define it: "Cultural development is both goal and process. It is a goal because it means

4

giving a society the ability to create its own life and environment. This ability means participation. But the process of cultural development entails more than participation alone. To be meaningful, such participation must be critical and continue to feed the sources of change."[6]

The conscious goals of Canadian federal administrations since 1867 have been national unity and economic prosperity. In time, the goal of fostering national identity was added, though cautiously and with little effort and small resources. Perhaps only the armed forces have understood from the start the importance of developing a sense of identity and the connection of culture with morale and community relations. Bands, retreats and tattoos have from early days been part of their routine; since the First World War official historians, war artists, the conscious collection of written and photographic records of the forces, and theatrical ventures have been included in their budgets.[7] The actor Raymond Massey began his career when he organized a minstrel show for the Canadian Expeditionary Force in Vladivostok in 1918.[8]

The bearing of culture on the original goals of public policy has only gradually begun to occupy the foreground of national attention. Little by little the writers and artists and musicians, formerly forgotten or disdained as idlers and dreamers, have begun to be perceived as creators of the symbols of integration.

Not everyone sees them that way. Many Canadians still view the arts the way a Victorian archbishop looked at them in the 1850s. Such things, wrote Archbishop Trench about music, painting and sculpture, are "the ornamental fringe of a people's life," and "can never, without loss of all manliness of character, be its main texture and woof – not to say that excellence in them has been too often dissociated from all true virtue and moral worth."[9] The disorderly lives of artists have

5

shocked more than Anglican prelates. A century later the Catholic bishop of Rimouski declared it would be sinful for Catholics to see the Royal Winnipeg Ballet, which was performing in his city for the first time. Against such opinions one might set the view of a Renaissance artist, Giorgio Vasari, who concluded four hundred years earlier, in his *Lives of the Artists*, "that the origin of the arts was nature itself, and that the first image or model was the beautiful fabric of the world, and that the master who taught us was that divine light infused in us by special grace, which has made us not only superior to the animal creation, but even, if one may say so, like God himself."[10]

My first professor of English literature at the University of Manitoba, Roy Daniells, discussing the cultural history of Canada at the Royal Society, quotes from the Arabian Nights what the Caliph said to Hassan: "Ah, if there shall ever arise a nation whose people have forgotten poetry or whose poets have forgotten the people, though they send their ships round Taprobane and their armies through the hills of Hindostan, though their city be greater than Babylon of old, though they mine a league into the earth or mount to the stars on wings – what of them?" And Hassan replied: "They will be a dark patch upon the world."[11]

The life of nations depends not only on its military and technical skill but also on its artists and chansonniers and poets. Every Pole can recite at least the opening lines of Mickiewicz's *Pan Tadeusz*, the Portuguese celebrate their national day on the birthday of their poet Camoëns, the Czechs were inspired to independence by that outrageously funny novel, Hašek's *The Good Soldier Schweik*, the Irish by the great writers of their literary renaissance. Yugoslavia owes its existence at least partly to the vision of its poet Njegŏs, the Prince-Archbishop of Montenegro, though no doubt his valour in killing Turks was equally inspiring. And we may remember that Mao Tse-tung and Ho Chi Minh were also poets.

The French have long understood the importance of their culture, and French Canadians have probably understood its function in nation-building better than most English-speaking Canadians. This may well be one of the things that continues to divide us. For years the English-Canadian attitude seems to have been that of Lord Melbourne, who said in 1835, "God help the Minister who meddles with art," a reluctance to make policy for a subject which seemed outside the competence of practical men.[12]

But a policy for the arts or a policy for culture need not, and should not meddle with art, any more than a policy for science need meddle with science. A distinction should be made. Art and artists, science and scientists, view the world in the light of imagination; what art or science is in itself is a matter for artists and scientists and critics to argue about. Government policy exists in the world of practical affairs, and purports to view reality in the light of reason. A policy for cultural development does not set out to regulate culture but to improve the conditions in which it can flourish, taking account of the ways in which citizens and governments and social scientists perceive it.

And here we run up against a remarkable shortage of the kind of information we need to have about the function of culture in our society, notwithstanding the amount of recent work that non-Canadian scholarship has yielded in the sociology of culture and other disciplines. I am thinking of the studies undertaken in England, France and in the United States, such as the recent one by the American National Committee for Cultural Resources surveying public attitudes to the work of a number of arts institutions in that country. For it is true,

7

as Lord Vaizey recently pointed out in England, that an analysis of box-office charges will hardly affect our opinion of *Così Fan Tutti*. But it is certainly not irrelevant to a study of the function of art or of the ways in which it is used and perceived. The arts in Britain, Lord Vaizey concludes, and especially the performing arts, take place in a fog of ignorance.[13]

I am not forgetting the illuminating if all too rare approach to the subject which Professor John Meisel contributed to the *Canadian Journal of Political Science* in December 1974. Professor Meisel drew attention to the cultural consequences of certain political decisions, stressing that we need to know a great deal more about the reciprocal relation between culture and politics.[14]

That there is such a relation is clear enough. A capitalist or a socialist or a mixed economy, being itself expressive of what is culturally normative and acceptable, has significant influence on the cultural environment of the society in question. The dominant sector – private or public – through the techniques of propaganda or advertising has obvious effects on values and lifestyles. So we need to know more about the relations between the economy and culture.

Without this knowledge there is no way of foreseeing the probable effects in the cultural area of decisions made in the economy or the polity.[15] Even cultural decisions, as we shall see, have a way of achieving the opposite effect from what was intended. This is beginning to be better understood, perhaps, in the context of native cultures and ecology than in urban contexts.

What is the function, for instance, of art in the community? One view of it was expressed in 1921 by Sir Edmund Walker, the first chairman of the National Gallery. He saw it as educational. "Canadian education, like education elsewhere," he said, "requires a close study of art at all times, because art is so closely interwoven with

8

the history of nations and the geography of countries, and the story of its growth is the story of all that is intellectual and moral."[16] That, no doubt, is much too large a claim even for so staunch an Anglophile in the Canada of 1921, but Sir Edmund was trying to make a point, the point about the essential character of the arts and culture to the development of a sense of nationhood. An eminent bank president, he was chairman and founder of several Canadian culture institutions. Among the group of rich private patrons who led the way in support of the arts he showed rare insight and imagination in the personal support he was to bring to Canada's museums, galleries and professional societies of artists. Perhaps he was ahead of his time, for he was unable to achieve much in the way of moving government to action in spite of his wealth and his influence with prime ministers.

Because men like Sir Edmund patronized "fine art," some commentators take the view that the function of art is elitist, ignoring the efforts of such patrons to insinuate culture into the daily life of the community. And while it is true that art can be used (or the patronage of art can be used) to enhance social status,[17] the notion that culture itself may be elitist seems to trouble many minds, forgetful that there are cultures in which art is not used in this way. Perhaps it is time to attempt a definition of culture.

Before I come to grips with a definition of culture as an area of government policy, let me say that I understand it to include science, but that in order to bring the discussion within manageable limits I shall concentrate on the subject matter with which, by training and experience, I am most familiar. And secondly I should say (and this is part of our dilemma as Canadians) that I write from the perspective of an English-speaking Canadian of a particular ethnic group, but have tried my best to view the problems in a comprehensive way. That my view is less comprehensive than it might have been will be evident, but in the absence of scholarly studies from Canadian universities or critics, and of reliable analyses of cultural data by federal and provincial government agencies, I have attempted only an essay, not an academic tome or a Cabinet document.

The word "culture" is notoriously ambiguous, all the more so because everyone imagines he knows exactly what he means by it; and this leads to arguments – not the good kind that clarify issues, but the bad kind where antagonists misunderstand one another and spend vast energy rebutting what was never asserted. Arguments about elitism versus radicalism and nationalism versus continentalism are often of this kind.

The thought of those ignorant armies clashing by night recalls Matthew Arnold.[18] One could begin with the notion of culture set forth in his *Culture and Anarchy*: the pursuit of sweetness and light, of the perfection of all that is best in human thought and imagination, epitomized for Arnold in the art and mind of ancient Greece. The quest for this culture is hindered by people Arnold called barbarians and philistines. He attacks the political expression of their dullness in the England of his day. The link between their politics and their culture was plain. There was a lot of new money in England, cruelly got and coarsely displayed; the contrast between the glory that was Greece and the banality that was suburbia was nowhere more blatant. In France too it obsessed the genius of Gustave Flaubert, whose *Dictionary of Received Ideas* is a kind of litany of bourgeois stupidities, elitist if you like; against it he sets the sombre magnificence of Hannibal's Carthage in *Salammbo*, the novel that expresses Flaubert's idea of nobility.

To define culture in a Canadian context, one might start with an English visitor to Montreal in the

10

1880s. In the poem "O God! O Montreal!" Samuel Butler describes a visit to the Montreal Museum of Natural History where he found (says the poem) two plaster casts of classical Greek sculpture banished to a storeroom where there was an old man stuffing an owl. Butler complains that the old man prefers the gospel of Montreal to the gospel of Hellas, condemning him to hellfire because the wretch calls trousers pants, though he has the excuse that Montreal is too busy with commerce to care about Greek masterpieces.[19]

Like Arnold, Butler was the product of a privileged classical education that stressed the superiority of Hellenic culture; like Arnold again, he was the son of a headmaster of a great public school (Arnold of Rugby, Butler of Shrewsbury). Both writers were steeped in the values of the British upper class, including their disdain for people in trade. Butler admired Greek sculpture, perhaps, because it was admired by this class. For all his love of beauty and truth, Butler's standard is first of all elitist, his view of culture too ethnocentric to allow him to see how often the arts have flourished in a commercial atmosphere. His ancient Greeks were themselves vigorous traders. Venice, Florence, Amsterdam and London refute him.

Are we to say, then, that the pursuit of perfection under some ideal form is no more than elitist, a kind of class snobbery? I think not. I would like to see it as one point on a circle of meanings. At the opposite pole is the anthropologists' sense of culture as the behaviour distinguishing a particular group.

There is no need to adopt an exclusive definition of culture. All its meanings are connected. For the pursuit of perfection, the definition of perfection, the type and message of cultural expression are all largely determined by the acquired behaviour distinguishing a particular social group. Again, the word "elitism" is not abso-

11

lute, but always associated with class or some kind of exclusiveness: to the factory worker the shop steward represents one elite; to the shop steward the union boss represents another; to the union boss the chairman of the board stands for yet another. Acknowledging that there is much to be said for and against defining culture as broadly as I have, in this study I shall take the meaning of the word culture to include: (1) artistic and creative expression, or expressive symbolism; (2) mores, manners and customs; (3) ethnicity; and (4) the social behaviour distinguishing groups.

At the core of all these ideas of culture is the notion of human imagination, the creative mind. The realm of imagination is limited only by the bounds of desire and revulsion, its laws are not those of reason; and this may explain why culture until very recently has seemed to those who create it to be intractable to social science, which seeks to be rational. The ability to create and invent, and respond to creation and invention, is born in everyone. Chomskian linguistics, for example, asserts that the capacity to invent new sentences is innate in everyone. True, there are some who have the gift of the gab, but all can create sentences never spoken before.

Talent, of course, does not exist in everyone. It is, as we say, a gift – that is, something given rather than acquired by learning and training, though it needs cultivation. In the art of writing, according to American novelist Walker Percy,[20] this gift is a kind of knack, like the ability to blow smoke through one's ears, something we find one person can do comparatively easily and another cannot. It is not simply the universal capacity for making sentences raised to an uncommon level. It is a kind of anomaly. And so with the other arts and sciences which require more or less cultivation. The incidence of talent in a population is probably fairly constant, like the incidence of psychosis, but the chances for its cultivation are unevenly distributed. If a society does not value a particular talent, it is likely to go undeveloped.

Governments should do nothing to confine or cramp these creative powers. On the contrary, cultural policy should seek to set them free. That is why it is essential for governments and people alike to perceive and understand the vital importance of human imagination and its expression in art and science. And not merely because its expression in commerce and industrial invention will follow, though that alone would justify the concern of governments. Even material culture has its origins in imagination; nothing in an automobile, for example, is found in nature. Even money is imaginary. For we not only live by imagination, by the myths and dreams that link us to our past and our environment, but we live *together* by imagination. "The glories of our blood and state/ Are shadows, not substantial things," the seventeenth-century English poet James Shirley wrote; they are none the less real for that.

Indeed they are often perceived as more real than reality. A great many Canadians are more concerned about the behaviour of the imaginary people in books and films and television than they are about concrete social issues. Images of violence on television have enough reality to warrant investigation by governments and their agencies; and the bad language of an imaginary character in a book prescribed for study in schools can plunge whole communities into controversy. That such agitations may be irrational is not the point. The point is that they demonstrate vividly the power and immediacy of images and symbols. This is well understood in political life, too, where personalities take pains – and spend money – to enhance their images, that is, their effect on the imagination of voters. "Culture gives people their view of reality,"[21] as the reality of peoples' environments helps mould their culture.

13

In its origins, the Canadian Confederation owed as much to the imagination and eloquence of figures like D'Arcy McGee as it did to the logic of politics, finance and commerce. It began, as all great human enterprises begin, with a dream. This dream became a reality by a political act. But the effects of the British North America Act were not just political. They were also economic, military, legal, social and, though the Fathers may not have considered the possibility, cultural. Every government decision, every public action, entails cultural implications. Either it affects the quality of life for some citizens or some community, as when an airport or a pipeline is constructed, or it touches in some way the national integrity, the imaginative bonds, the symbols that unite or divide us. There will be such effects whether the action is in the polity, the economy or the social structure. In the words of Jacques Rigaud, assistant director general of UNESCO: "To guarantee that culture is taken into account as societies make decisions, it must figure as an integral part of any social plan, one not imposed on, but rather proposed to, the public."[22]

That is a perception with which I am fully sympathetic, but however you may wish to define the word culture and whatever relationship you see it having with the "substantial" responsibilities of government, how did Canadians first see the place of culture in their society or at least develop those habits of mind that determine the culture in which we now live, and how have we and our governments come to view it?

14

Along the whole of the north shore I did not see one cartload of earth and yet I landed in many places. . . . I am rather inclined to believe that this is the land God gave to Cain.
                                        Jacques Cartier, 1534.

I wish the British Government would give you Canada at once. It is fit for nothing but to breed quarrels.
                                        Alexander Baring to John Quincy Adams, U.S. Ambassador to the Court of St. James, 1816.

England would be better off without Canada; it keeps her in a prepared state for war at a great expense and constant irritation.
                                        Napoleon I, 1817.

Canada must neither be lost nor given away!
                                        William IV (1830-37)

The cold narrow minds, the confined ideas, the by-gone prejudices of the society are hardly conceivable, books there are none, nor music, and as for pictures! – the Lord deliver us from such! The people do not know what a picture is.
                                        Anna Jameson, 1837.

I have little doubt that the French, when once placed, by the legitimate course of events and the working of natural courses, in a minority, would abandon their vain hope of nationality.
                                        Lord Durham, 1839.

Advancing quietly; old differences settling down and being fast forgotten; – health and vigour throbbing in its steady pulse: it is full of hope and promise.
                                        Charles Dickens, 1842.

Is there a man amongst us who forgets that when Papineau was struggling for the rights of his race and for the constitutional liberty which we today enjoy, his principal coadjutors were John Nelson, the Scotchman, and O'Callaghan, the Irishman?
                                        Sir Wilfrid Laurier, 1877.

TWO

The Canadian tradition, at the time of Confederation, was already one of cultural freedom (a cynic might call it cultural neglect), a mental habit that grew out of the compromises made early in our history between traders and native people, and between French Catholics and British Protestants.

The history of culture in Canada begins with our physical environment and our native peoples and it continues with the invasions of North America by European empires. These more recent events are often discussed in terms of conquest and exploitation, and such language is surely justified. But it tends to distract us from noticing that the conquerors were changed by those they exploited, if not as much as their subjects were changed by them at least to a significant degree. Harold Innis in his seminal work on the fur trade has shown that this reciprocity of influences – in effect an exchange of technologies – was particularly true of Canada, where the conditions of the fur trade bred a certain mutual tolerance.[1] There was a good deal of misunderstanding at the level of symbolic culture. The martyrdom of Brébeuf and his brethren is only one example; there must have been many martyrs to the old Indian religions, as there were untold barbaric acts against natives by the "civilized." At the material level, though, the Indians needed European trade goods – guns, axes, kettles and the like, in addition to the "trinkets" of popular cliché. (Trinkets, I suppose, is the name one gives to other people's luxury goods.) The Europeans needed luxury and military goods of their own, mainly furs for beaver hats and coarser beaver hair to reinforce armour.

But the exchange went beyond that. To survive in the harsh country of the Precambrian Shield, trader-explorers had to adopt the tools, skills and habits of the natives: birchbark canoe, snowshoe, pemmican diet. The shocks of culture contact were sometimes eased by sex. Samuel Hearne learned the art of Arctic travel from women; even the doughty Sir George Simpson did not disdain their consolation.[2]

This need to learn from the natives was sometimes felt as a threat to identity: the authorities in New France made frequent attempts to stop young colonists from running wild in the woods. But the call of the wild was strong and the *coureurs de bois* increased in numbers despite restraints. As everywhere else in the world, there was conflict between the demands of settlement and the nomadic habits of trappers and hunters. The French had come to Canada for a mixture of reasons – political, commercial, scientific and religious. Private motives were often different, including the passion for the free life of the lakes and forests. Official, rather than popular, disapproval of the *coureurs de bois* was to drive Des Groseilliers and Radisson into the arms of their enemies the English.

From a cultural point of view, what is interesting about the English trading that began on the shores of Hudson Bay in 1668 was its replacement of the proselyt-

18

izing motive represented by the Bishop in New France with the new, scientific spirit of the Royal Society. The French too had brought science and Cartesian mathematics to the new world, but traces of these disciplines in seventeenth-century North America are faint. The creators of the Hudson's Bay Company included several members of the Royal Society, eminent figures like Robert Boyle (of Boyle's Law) and Sir Christopher Wren. "You are to keep exact journals," the company's servants were repeatedly told (though here too the Jesuits' *Relations* had pointed the way). "You are to use the natives with kindness and civility" was another favourite injunction. Considering the sectarian passions of the seventeenth century, with its faith in the maxim *Cuius regio, eius religio* (the rulers' religion is the peoples') it şeems amazing that the English made little attempt until much later to spread the Protestant gospel from their forts by the frozen sea, until one remembers that if the Indians had given up their own nomadic cultures they would have stopped the hunting and trapping that brought in the furs.

Dependent in this way on native hunters, many of the fur traders learned the Indian languages and came to admire their cultures – and to leave them be. True, Indians and Inuit suffered the shocks and traumas of culture contact with the rival imperial powers and their technology and were decimated by new diseases against which they had no resistance. True, their traditional cultures were changed and modified; there is no such thing, after all, as a culture or a language that remains frozen in its archaic form and still lives. But the integrity of Amerindian cultures was never destroyed. During the long reign of the fur trade in the Shield country, tribal cultures managed to adapt to the invading value systems. This state of affairs, Innis points out, did not prevail in areas such as the United States or the fertile regions of

19

the Canadian Northwest after settlers began to pour in. In Canada the habit of using the natives with something like kindness and civility persisted just enough to modify the violence too common in the western development of North America.

In the greatest museums of Amerindian cultures, in Paris, London, New York and Ottawa, in the writings of the renowned anthropologist Claude Lévi-Strauss, in the statements of one of America's most celebrated contemporary painters, the late Barnett Newman, the glory of these cultures is hailed in phrases normally reserved for the legacies of Greece and Rome. But the evidence of the survival of Amerindian cultures is not in museums alone but rather in that, after three centuries of stress, they are undergoing renewal everywhere. Meanwhile anthropology, the child of imperialism and exploration, has taught white men to respect cultures that are not their own, if only in theory. The only remaining threat to native cultures is contemporary technology – which threatens all cultures.

The culture of English-speaking Canada, then, is secular and scientific in its origins. Attempts to establish an official religion failed. The culture of French Canada began with apostolic and aristocratic tendencies; little heed was paid the scientific commentaries of Cartier and Champlain. The Governor looked after the politics and external relations of New France, the Intendant after the civil administration and economy and the Bishop after the religion – an important part of culture. In the 1690s Governor Frontenac had attempted to have Molière's comedy *Tartuffe* performed in Québec, and the Bishop banned it. The great patron of the arts in France was Le Roi Soleil, Louis XIV, for whom artists existed like the Hall of Mirrors in his great palace of Versailles to multiply images of his splendour. The King did not need clergy to improve his taste. But in the new world the

Bishop had his say. Yet it was the Church that brought European ecclesiastical art to the new world. Nothing could be more striking than the magnificence of Québec's early churches, set down as they were in the wilderness, asserting the faith of pioneering habitants. As early as 1668, Bishop Laval set up a school for arts and crafts at St-Joachim at Cap Tourmente.[3] Masters like Jacques Leblond and Frère Luc brought their skills from France.

To begin with, sculpture, particularly the vigorous and distinctive wood sculpture, was the supreme art, seconded by votive painting. The domestic and decorative arts – furniture-making, silver-smithing, fabric-weaving and embroidery – did not flourish until there was a prosperous class outside the Church to patronize them. And by that time some of the most unique and promising crafts had withered or died.

The point I want to emphasize is that Canadian cultural habits as they existed in 1867 have their origins in the seventeenth and eighteenth centuries, when the Catholic Church and the imperial corporations engaged in the fur trade brought European culture into the new world. Conflicts which elsewhere caused frightful misery (in Ireland, for example, under the Penal Laws) were much less violent in Canada. Years before there was religious toleration in the British Isles, the Québec Act gave it to French Canada. Not long after the Conquest, for example, the Catholic Bishop in Québec City placed his church at the disposal of the Anglicans until they obtained one of their own. The first British governors never dreamed of assaulting the French language. Newfoundland was permitted a Catholic bishop in 1776, if only because the British had reached a working accommodation with the hierarchy in nearby Québec; he was later given a government pension as a reward for his help in averting a mutiny of the garrison. A Catholic elected to the Nova Scotia Assembly in 1823 was allowed to take his seat. Canadians ignored or rejected the bourgeois revolutions in France and America. And though there were, relatively speaking, significant rebellions in the Canadian provinces in the 1830s they struck little fire from either their English- or French-speaking countrymen as similar movements did in Western Europe in the same decade. It is true that anti-Catholic bigotry was strong in Protestant Canada and that riots and fights between Orangemen and Catholics took place regularly, sometimes attended by fatalities. It was this kind of bigotry that led to the execution of Louis Riel and was a factor in the enactment of the Manitoba Schools Act. But as a rule, the sectarian factions were careful not to go too far. As with the tensions between natives and traders, hostility was mollified by an awareness of common interests, though it cannot be denied that too often the culture of majorities prevailed.

In the years following the Métis rebellion in Saskatchewan under Riel, Canada became a country whose heroes were policemen, the redcoats of the Royal Canadian Mounted Police. A nation's habits create a nation's symbols; if events like those surrounding Riel persist, they become dangerous symbols of bigotry that undermine the capacity of a community to remain intact and healthy.

Cultural habits grew from the choices made by pioneering Canadians; from the ways in which newcomers learned from earlier inhabitants; and from the ways in which they dealt with the environment, with conflicting imperialisms, with conflicting religions, with the clash of ideologies and interests. The French-Canadian culture as defined since the 1840s by Parent, Garneau and others, was embedded in a soil, a history, a language ("nos institutions, notre langue et nos lois"), all strengthening a particular set of habits, tastes, styles.[4] Habits of interdependence, freedom and mutual toleration may be found from the early days in the Iroquois Confederacy, whose constituent tribes kept their distinctive character within the organization of the Five Nations. Such habits are probably unconscious, but taken together they amount to a distinctive national, rather than regional, character. And such habits were not lost on the imagination of the Canadian political leaders of the 1860s who decided to try to build not one country from one British colony but a nation of nations from several colonies. What was lost by French and English descendants of the Conquest, alike, was an understanding that time cannot heal the wound of conquest. For the descendants of the conquered the painful reality of an imperial defeat was transformed over generations into a deeply subconscious sense of national hurt and injustice; for the descendants of the conquerors a pleasant fact of history was transformed into a subconscious sense of superiority.

The new federation created in 1867 by the British North America Act relied on the unifying influence of the transcontinental railroad. The cultural effects of the railroad (in terms of the way Canadians would come to see themselves) had not been foreseen. The Métis of the prairies, who had not been consulted, bitterly resented the sale of the Hudson's Bay Company's territory to the Dominion. The railroad bringing settlers to their ranges would destroy their free nomadic life. The same railroad made it comparatively easy to bring troops to the region and enforce native submission. Advancing technology has always posed a threat to the habits of developing communities.

Along with the railroad came the extension of the telegraph system, which too might have been expected to act as a unifying influence. Instead, it was divisive. And before long it, too, had the opposite effect. As early as 1896, the historian W. E. H. Lecky in his book *Democracy and Liberty* had this to say:

> The growth of an independent provincial spirit has been much accelerated by the telegraph. The political influence of this great invention, though various and chequered, has been scarcely less powerful than that of the railway. It has brought the distant dependencies of the Empire into far closer connection with the mother country; but it is very doubtful whether the power it has given to the home ministers of continually meddling with the details of their administration is a good thing, and there have been times of disagreement when a rapid communication between foreign countries might have led rather to war than peace. Government by telegraph is a very dangerous thing. . . . The effect, however, on which I would now specially dwell is its great power in *decentralising* politics. The provincial press, no doubt, owes much to the repeal of the stamp duty and paper duty, but the immense development and importance it has assumed within the lifetime of men who are still of middle age are mainly due to the existence of telegraphic communications.[5]

Lecky goes on to point out that the telegraph put an end to the metropolitan advantage of priority of information. It is tempting to see in this passage the seeds of the later Harold Innis, in his work on communications and empire which was to influence Marshall McLuhan.[6] For the moment it is enough to observe that every subsequent acceleration of communication in Canada, created and financed to bind the country together more closely, to help the flow of trade and information, and make the

24

regions interdependent, has also entailed the unforeseen effect of strengthening Canada's regional character. It has contributed instead to preventing not only the emergence of a national metropolis but also of a deeper sense of community. And the process has not stopped. Not only in Canada, but all over the world, regional nationalisms are resurgent.

From its beginnings, as we have seen, the emerging Canadian culture was in touch with universal ideas – ideas represented by the Catholic Church and the Enlightenment. Throughout the nineteenth century Europe was developing the doctrine of nations. The Italian writer Vico defined a nation as "a natural society of men who by unity of territory, of origin, of customs and of language, are drawn into a community of life and social conscience." This idea of nationality, stretching back to Dante and earlier, was to inspire the reunification of Italy and the rise of a German empire. The right of nations, so understood, was widely believed to include political independence. The Americans certainly believed this and proved it to their liking. The Swiss federation had emphatically rejected this doctrine. The Canadian Confederation largely ignored it, intent on linking together in a single political unit colonies that had already developed a consciousness of their own and were in a sense distinct nations and cultures.

In the great migrations of the nineteenth and early twentieth centuries, successive waves of immigrants brought their traditions to Canada. The Irish were energetic leaders in the struggle for responsible government and the rights of religious minorities; their Catholic benevolent societies and Orange lodges were pioneers in social organization, the forerunners of trade unions and political party groupings. They brought eloquence to journalism and politics, and song and conviviality to the sober townships. The Germans brought their steadiness

25

and intellectual strength. The Eastern Europeans who came to the prairies early in this century gave a mystical colour to their region as well as a lot of sweat to their new employers. They formed the audiences that filled the theatres of western cities, not seeking ghetto culture but Shakespeare in Yiddish. Hugh MacLennan has paid tribute to the more recent European immigrants who taught a new sophistication to Montreal and Toronto.[7] Canadians of earlier vintage were able to accommodate them all, however ungraciously at times. But the changes they had brought were not fully or easily understood.

In 1891 an editorial in *Saturday Night* magazine asked, "Why did Wolfe take the trouble to fight Montcalm? Was it not to make the Anglo-Saxon supreme?" Its views on recent immigrants were firm. Of Jews it said, "Their sole idea of making a living is to barter in refuse, skulk through city lanes and operate on a business level that the native race will not descend to." As for the Chinese, "Let them swarm in once and the yellow stain on the country will be one that cannot be rubbed out." And the black man was "by nature unfit for carving out a home for himself in the wilderness." As late as the 1920s *Saturday Night* was sure that Canada was "white man's country."[8] This was the voice of Protestant Toronto, Hog Town to many Canadians in the years before and shortly after the First World War. But it was not alone in failing either to recognize and understand the plight of cultural minorities seeking to adapt to the established habits of a new majority and environment, or to distinguish the nature of their suffering from those French in Québec who had become a submerged majority. Bad habits become bad symbols and are as easily developed as good ones in the life of peoples.

Education, the transmission of culture from generation to generation, was reserved as a subject of legislation to the provinces, and while this seemed proper and necessary in a country with two dominant languages and many cultures, it has posed drastic problems, notably in its failure to impart a sense of common history.[9] This was noted by Lord Durham in the nineteenth century, and by others since, whose political prescriptions and proposals have not proven too successful. Divisive myths have grown unchecked, including the myth that the provinces are in Confederation only on conditions, and that the constitution of Canada is a kind of treaty between nations which can be broken at will. Meanwhile the memory of the great events in which Canadians have taken part together as a community was allowed to fade.

This cultural effect of the bold political design of Confederation had not been foreseen, particularly by its draftsmen. And though there was, and is, a clear need for federal cultural policy to make good the defect, Ottawa neglected to provide it in any energetic way before the middle of the twentieth century.

This neglect is difficult to understand when one realizes how much more complicated the cultural problem had become in the century following Durham's Report. Federal awareness of the importance of the issue one might have thought would have become obvious to political leaders. It had not. They consistently failed to recognize that the cultural issue in Canada is more complex and requires more attention as a continuing political problem than is the case in most other countries. Canada, as they knew, had had the cultures of Western Europe, first French and then British, imposed upon a North American environment to which they were entirely alien. Because of the superior technology of these alien European cultures, the French and British were able to submerge the aboriginal cultures of the Indian and Inuit peoples, though the Europeans never did succeed in suppressing these native cultures completely. The Conquest led to retreat of the French back to France and of the

27

French Canadian into himself; but the British victors did not try consciously to destroy the development of Québécois culture. After 1867 there were continuing and cyclical waves of immigration from other regions of Europe and Asia, each group bringing to this country its own sense of cultural conflict with the compatriots it had left behind and its suspicions of the North Americans it encountered in the new world. Thus, these layers of potential conflict – this palimpsest of fermenting explosive materials dating back in time to the traditional British-French rivalries of the Norman conquest, of the Seven Years' and the Napoleonic Wars, to the martyrdom and exploitation by which European values were imposed on aboriginal cultures, to the real conflicts of descendants of the Conquest, of the United Empire Loyalists, of the Battle of the Boyne, of Chinese railroad workers, or of Russian Mennonites – were left to fester by successive Canadian administrations.

This reluctance of Canadian political leaders to become involved in the cultural fears and fortunes of the changing faces of Canada was probably an inheritance from Britain. The last British sovereign who was an effective patron of the arts was Charles I; his immediate successors were the Puritans, who not only chopped off his head but dispersed his collections. The visual arts, they believed, were tainted with popery, and the performing arts were sinful. Despite the revival of theatre at the Restoration, the Puritans bequeathed their suspicion of the arts to the common people of Britain. This Puritan antagonism was imported into Canada and may still be one of the lingering obstacles to government support for the arts.

The federal government was uncertain whether "culture" was part of "education," a provincial responsibility: the word culture never appeared in the constitution. There may also have been doubts about the principle concerning the competence of any government in cultural matters, as there were in Britain until after the middle of the nineteenth century. Janet Minihan points out that in Britain, "In the 1820s, the state's responsibilities were held to begin and end with administering justice, collecting taxes and defending the country.... That the state had any responsibility for the living artist would have seemed ludicrous to most Englishmen, not only in the 1820s, but throughout most of the century." When Benjamin Haydon, the painter, wrote to the Duke of Wellington in 1830 suggesting that the government set aside one or two thousand pounds a year for the arts, the Tory Prime Minister replied: "The Duke is convinced that Mr. Haydon's good sense will point out to him the impossibility of doing what he suggests."[10] Haydon had no better luck in 1835 with the Whig Prime Minister, Lord Melbourne, whose remark about meddling in the arts has already been quoted.

I have argued that support for the arts need not take the form of meddling. But there is always a danger, even in democratic countries, that those who distribute funds for the arts will be tempted to interfere in their use, indulging their personal taste or, worse, their political bias. This temptation is particularly dangerous in a country like Canada, where national unity cannot be regarded as a foregone conclusion and where a one-party-dominated federal party system has tended to endow the governing party with a sense that the Opposition can rarely act in the public interest. The capricious notions of politicians at the ministerial level are no substitute for parliamentary legislation or publicly discussed policies, especially in a system where parliamentarians have few opportunities to challenge ministerial decisions successfully.

However, a good deal was achieved before the First World War without meddling. In Britain, music and

29

the performing arts were, for the most part, supported by public attendance until well into the twentieth century. The earliest forms of government support for the arts, as distinct from royal patronage, involved the establishment of museums and art galleries. The British Museum was founded in 1753. In France, the Louvre was opened to the public as a museum in 1793. In the United States, Congress established the Smithsonian Institution in 1846, eleven years after the bequest by James Smithson for the foundation of an "establishment for the increase & diffusion of Knowledge among men." In Canada, the first involvement was in the tentative beginnings of the National Museum from a collection of specimens by the Geological Survey, following organized pressure on the united parliament of 1841 from the Natural History Society of Montreal and the Literary and Historical Society of Québec.[11]

In Britain, despite the unbending disapproval of Wellington and Melbourne, the government was already involved in support for culture. The foundation of the British Museum had been prompted by the chance to acquire several important collections of books, manuscripts, and natural history specimens, the funds being raised by a public lottery. The government, once involved, could not avoid putting up money for a building, which led to the purchase of other collections, such as the Elgin marbles in 1816, to prevent their being dispersed or taken out of the country. Similar motives led to the purchase in 1824 of the Angerstein collection as the foundation of the National Gallery, which was established in London in 1827 but did not become totally independent of the British Museum until about 1855.

The British upper classes, in their private capacity, did more for the development and dissemination of the arts than is commonly admitted. In addition to those who acquired large collections and opened them to the public,

30

there were many who believed that, in the absence of a national educational system, one of the best ways to increase the contentment and improve the taste of the lower orders was to make it possible for them to view the wonders of nature and the works of man in museums and art galleries. They seem to have hit on a good idea, for in 1846, for example, 825,091 people visited the British Museum and 608,140 went to the National Gallery.[12]

Another argument for cultural development which was neglected by the British government, until its hand was forced by private citizens, many of them noblemen, was that exposure to the fine arts was good for trade, in that it tended to improve design and so promote exports. The Society of Arts, which had been founded in 1754 by a group of noblemen and gentlemen but had become more or less moribund, was revived in the late 1840s and organized a series of industrial exhibitions, which attracted crowds of up to 100,000 persons. These led directly to the highly successful and popular Great Exhibition of 1851, presided over by the Prince Consort. It had been privately financed, the government doing no more than provide some facilities at no charge. Its catalogue remarked: "The success which has attended the enterprise may, in a great measure, be referred to the freedom of action which this dissociation from the timid councils of the government secured for its projectors."[13] One immediate outcome was the establishment, in 1852, of a Department of Practical Art within the Board of Trade, later expanded into a Department of Science and Art under the Board of Education. Profits from the Exhibition were used to acquire land in South Kensington and to build the Victoria and Albert and other museums that are still there today.[14]

The influence of Queen Victoria's husband, the Prince Consort, extended into Canada; for their daughter, Princess Louise, was the wife of the Marquess of

Lorne, who when Governor General of Canada was the moving spirit in founding the Royal Canadian Academy and the National Gallery of Canada in 1880. Behind his significant initiative was a group of Canadian artists led by the painter Lucius R. O'Brien.[15] The British National Gallery was inadequately housed for many years, and the restless life of the National Gallery of Canada suffered a similar fate, suggesting that art was one of the neglected children of Confederation, farmed out as an ephemeral guest of government departments like Fisheries or the Supreme Court.

The Gallery began with an exhibition at the Clarendon Hotel, Sussex Street, Ottawa, under the authority of the Department of Public Works. In 1907 Sidney Fisher, Minister of Agriculture and Public Works, won Parliament's approval for the establishment of an Arts Advisory Council. George Reid, president of the Royal Canadian Academy, had urged the Laurier government to let the Academy appoint a committee of artists who, with other "laymen" and a full-time director, would strengthen the Gallery's position and role. However, he ran into opposition from Governor General Lord Grey, who felt the Academy's grip on the young institution was already too tight. In the end, Fisher's announcement referred to a council of "gentlemen who have shown their interest in and appreciation and understanding of art as evidenced by their public connection with art associations and their private patronage of art," the same kind of trustees appointed to oversee the Gallery's operations today.[16]

In 1910 the National Gallery moved into the Victoria Memorial Museum Building along with the Geological Survey's National Museum; and Eric Brown, an important figure in the development of Canadian art, was appointed curator. Even when the National Gallery was incorporated under a Board of Trustees in 1913, the in-

32

creasingly valuable collection did not find a permanent home designed to accommodate it. But the 1916 fire in the Parliament Buildings drove Commons and Senate to take over the new museum and the Gallery's collection went into storage. Turning disaster to advantage, the Gallery began its policy of sending out touring exhibitions.

The same hand-to-mouth existence was the lot of the federal Public Archives in Ottawa. In 1872 a small beginning had been made toward the collection and preservation of public records, with a parliamentary grant of $4,000 for the half-time services of a second-class clerk under the authority of the Department of Agriculture. (There seems to have been a tendency to confuse culture and agriculture.) In 1898 Dr. Douglas Brymer was appointed Dominion Archivist. It was a Governor General, Lord Minto, who convinced Sir Wilfrid Laurier of the importance of national archives, urging the appointment of Arthur C. Doughty, who became Dominion Archivist in 1904. Once again the impetus to support culture was aristocratic, egged on by a single-minded activist in the field or by a tiny group of professionals. D'Arcy McGee had said in 1865, "Patriotism will increase in Canada as its history is read."[17] As we have seen, Lord Minto and his friend Doughty found at the turn of the century that the history taught in Canadian schools was conflicting and divisive. Doughty, like Edmund Walker and others, believed a corrective would be better education centred on a sound historiography based firmly on documents. His work was applauded in Parliament in 1906 by the leader of the Opposition, Robert Borden, who pressed the government to give the Dominion Archivist adequate funds and a free hand. Prime Minister Laurier was not reluctant. He had told a friend, "My object is to consolidate Confederation and to bring out people, long estranged from each other, gradually to become a nation."

33

Doughty and his collaborator Adam Shortt saw their work as archivists as serving this end. In 1921 Sir Robert Borden was to return to the theme of his earlier plea to Laurier.

> Crops and manufactures do not make up the whole life of a nation. The development of the intellectual and spiritual qualities of the nation, of the moral qualities of the people, is surely not of less importance. A nation which neglects these higher considerations cannot hold its place in the world. The preservation of our records has a direct relation to such considerations.[18]

Canadian federal parliamentarians have rarely injected partisan politics into cultural issues.

But there is little evidence that even enlightened political leaders saw a connection between the need for public care of archives and the public care or patronage of living artists and writers. Poets had always need of patronage of one kind or another. It was different with other kinds of writers who, throughout the nineteenth century, had been made more or less independent of patronage by the rise of a new, literate middle class, particularly women, who had provided a market for books. But the rise of the novel is not only linked with the rise of this class but also in part, as the result of serialization by several popular magazines of the time, with the rise of the lower classes. The private patrons in Britain and France who in the eighteenth century had offered writers places in their households or, if they were in holy orders, ecclesiastical livings or sinecures had been replaced a hundred years later by publishers and their markets.

In Canada two distinct publishing centres, in Montreal and Toronto, were growing up in the early years of Confederation, in addition to a certain amount of regional publishing. British and American publishers, finding new and profitable markets for their books in English-speaking Canada, found it convenient to deal with Canadian publishers as their agents. A number of Toronto houses grew rich on the agency business; as "jobbers" they were primarily salesmen and tended to regard money spent on editorial effort as wasted. As the Canadian market grew, many British and American houses set up branches of their own.

It was hardly surprising that in this atmosphere Canadian letters were slow to develop. In compensation there was access to the ideas and, for some writers, the markets of the world. "Imperialism was one form of Canadian nationalism."[19] Though the notion may now seem strange, the imperial connection was a source of great pride to many Canadians, just as the United States was a magnet. "I ... am an Imperialist," Stephen Leacock said, "because I will not be a Colonial."[20] For French Canadians, less enthusiastic about their place in the empire on which the sun never set, and less interested in the cultural continentalism emerging in New York, the Catholic Church, with its access to the tradition of Christian humanism that went back to Erasmus, opened a window on Western civilization. And if the window was a narrow one, it may have been because the Church in Canada was tinged with *un rigorisme moral*. Still, there is evidence of a feeling of isolation in Canada in the nineteenth century, especially in the prairies and backwoods. There was, as Northrop Frye has said, a sense that the real action in human affairs was elsewhere.

It was a harsh climate for art and learning, as harsh as the natural environment with its empty distances that weighed on the imagination. Perhaps the most important consolation in North America was the institution and growth of public libraries, either by rich philanthrop-

35

ists and the trusts they were beginning to establish, or by municipalities. The name of Andrew Carnegie, whose beneficence extended to the establishment of public libraries in his native Scotland and in Canada, is pre-eminent.

The earliest libraries originated in the seventeenth century in Nova Scotia. Marc Lescarbot, Parisian scholar and advocate, decided to share his important private collection of books with his fellow Acadians in the Annapolis Basin soon after his arrival in 1606. Within two hundred and fifty years the most influential institutions and most powerful religious and political leaders helped establish a network of libraries from coast to coast. The Jesuits and the Hudson's Bay Company, John Graves Simcoe, Joseph Howe, Lord Dalhousie and Egerton Ryerson saw the value of constructing community centres of learning with the library as their focus. In Québec, the Cabinet de lecture paroissial and the Institut Canadien in Montréal and in Québec City had an enormous vogue which, when matched by the growth of the Québec Literary and Historical Society and the Société historique de Montréal, made a major contribution to intellectual development. The earliest Mechanics Institute was founded in 1827 in Newfoundland followed by others in Montréal in 1828, Toronto in 1830, Halifax in 1831 and Kingston in 1834. Many received grants from governments and the best became the nuclei of our most important university and public libraries of the twentieth century. Despite the promising initiatives involving the working class, Canadian labour did not concern itself much with cultural development.[21]

The turn of the century saw the birth of a number of provincial cultural institutions. In Québec a museum was opened in Laval University in 1876, the Musée du Séminaire de Québec; and in 1880 the province of Québec authorized a Museum of Public Instruction. The

Art Association of Montreal was founded in 1860, mainly acting as an exhibiting society until the turn of the century when it began to form its own collection. In 1876 the Montreal Museum of Fine Arts came into being under a benefaction from Benaiah Gibb. In 1872 the Ontario Society of Artists was established in Toronto. By 1912 the art school the Society had opened in 1876 had become the Ontario College of Art. In New Brunswick the Owens Art Gallery established itself at Mount Allison University in 1890.

In British Columbia the first recorded art exhibition was held in 1890 and in 1894 the Art, Historical and Scientific Association was founded and is still operating. Indeed, the turn of the century saw the flowering of a number of cultural institutions in British Columbia: the Vancouver Women's Musical Club [1915]; the Vancouver Symphony Society [1919]; the Shakespeare Society [1915]; the Vancouver Little Theatre Association [1921] ; the B.C. Arts League [1920]; and the Canadian Women's Press Club [1904].

Manitobans had had active theatre groups even before the formation of the province and by the turn of the century several chains of theatres had been constructed, the most famous being C. P. Walker's. And while most of the cultural institutions and organizations in the prairie province were created after the Second World War, several musical groups, including the Manitoba Musical Festival, were established before, in 1919 and the early twenties. In 1912 the Civic Art Gallery and Museum was sponsored by Winnipeg activists in the arts and it became the basic institution for teaching and ultimately exhibiting in this field. It was soundly rooted in the work of the Winnipeg Sketch Club founded in 1914 and the Manitoba Society of Artists established in 1920.

In 1912 the Hamilton Art Gallery was founded. In the early 1900s the University of Toronto's various collec-

37

tions became the nucleus of the Royal Ontario Museum, founded in 1914. Its new building was completed about the same time, following a campaign led by Sir Edmund Walker, with funds put up by a number of the city's wealthy citizens. The Art Museum of Toronto, founded in 1900, became the Art Gallery of Toronto, funded by some of the same people. It opened in 1913 in the Grange, former home of Goldwyn Smith. Hart Massey, whose Methodism did not exclude all forms of art, built Massey Hall as a centre for concerts.

The initiative of Toronto's millionaires reflected the elitist temper of the age and a desire to legitimize the possession of wealth. But no comparable initiative is to be found in francophone Québec. And this raises the question of patronage, of who paid or pays the artist. It is related to the question of the artist's function. In ages of faith, his function is to glorify God and magnify the Church. As faith declines, art becomes increasingly propagandist and emphatic, as in the Baroque art of the seventeenth century, as though to overwhelm doubt. The Church is the artist's patron, though increasingly the pious donor, prince or magnate, actually puts up the money, and in return receives his share of the glory.

In the next age the artist's function is to celebrate the magnificence of his prince, who rewards him with wealth and honours. With the rise of cities and their bourgeoisie, it is the rich man who becomes the artist's patron, in return for art that affirms his taste and confers a kind of legitimacy on his wealth. And so down to our own age with its art and architecture that celebrates the romantic self, through the storms and stresses of protean modernism, expressing the multitudinous individualism of self-realization and self-discovery – to the point where the American social critic Daniel Bell sees it at odds with a social structure that is increasingly impersonal and reified.[22] In this age the individualist finds his reward in the marketplace or else, as often as not, is not paid at all. But ours is also the age which has seen the rise of mass marketing, recruiting an army of writers and artists in the cause of selling imaginary goods. Here the arts themselves may petrify, losing their character as expressive symbolism.

But, in the seventeenth century, the patronage of the Governor, and particularly of the Bishop which had made possible the flowering of a unique style and quality of architecture and sculpture, nurtured the French derivative developments in painting, and supported the gradual evolution of superb craftsmanship in the domestic and decorative arts from silver to embroidery, was not replaced by the patronage of either the rich or the state in the eighteenth or nineteenth centuries. Imperial France could have helped but it had already deserted its former colony. By the time of Confederation, and indeed until the beginning of the Second World War, Canadian culture in Québec was perceived to be "English." True, folk art such as the weaving of *les ceintures fléchées* continued, but by the time Louis Jobin, the woodcarver of the Baillairgé school of Québec died in the mid-1920s, his death symbolized the end of another French-Canadian tradition. Self-taught artists like Ozias Leduc, a painter-chronicler such as Charles-Edouard Huot, a sculptor like Louis-Philippe Hébert and even the brilliant Québec cartoonist Henri Julien, depended for their inspiration less on Canada than on Paris, London or the environment of the immediate district into which they were born, and almost entirely for their livelihood on English or English-dominated institutions. There were exceptions, of course, particularly among poets like Octave Crémazie or Louis Fréchette at the beginning of the twentieth century or among writers like Henri Bourassa and Lionel Groulx later. But, by and large, and perhaps unnoticed by governments and most informed citizens the fragments of the culture of French Canada were almost totally dependent for their survival on the determination of a few talented individuals operating quite separately from the world of their English-Canadian colleagues (assisted by the continuing use of the French language and the efforts, albeit declining, of the Church).

One reason for the lack of continuity of patronage of the arts in Québec stemmed from the absence there (outside the Church) of the English tradition of voluntarism and, of course, of a strong middle class. It is not that there were no voluntary associations: there was the influential Société Saint-Jean-Baptiste and the Institut Canadien at first in Montréal and later in Québec (1842). But they were of less consequence when compared with the proliferation of voluntary societies in other parts of Canada, with their mushrooming cultural activities and the influence they were able to bring to bear on government and the rich. This role of the volunteer should not be overlooked because of the occasional dramatic initiatives of a few millionaires in Toronto, Vancouver or English Montréal. Pan-Canadian societies of professional artists or art supporters began to be formed. The Royal Canadian Institute was founded in 1849; the Royal Society of Canada in 1882, inspired partly by the example of the Royal Dublin Society; the Federal Women's Institutes of Canada in 1887; and the Imperial Order of Daughters of the Empire in 1900. There were many others. In the country as a whole, a growing sense of nationalism was leading to the formation of national organizations to represent an increasing number of professionals in the arts: the Canadian Handicrafts Guild (1906), the Royal Architectural Institute of Canada (1907), the Canadian Society of Painters in Water Colour (1925), to name only a few.

In Canada the "large, furry ladies" who welcomed visiting celebrities (the phrase is Dylan Thomas's) did much to keep their communities in touch with the best art, music and ideas of their time. They were rooted in those rural evenings in church basements where any visitor with a story to tell was welcome, while Mary-Ellen provided a tasteful interlude on the accordion and Jake the barber did his tap dance. The women who organized these affairs do not deserve all the gibes which this age of professionalism has flung at them.

Since culture is largely unconscious, as T. S. Eliot pointed out a few years ago in *Christianity and Culture*,[23] it is hardly surprising that the federal government in Canada was slow to foster it. Except in the Department of National Defence, federal incursions into patronage or supportive legislation were the result of isolated initiatives until the end of the Second World War.

The bearing of culture on morale was well understood in Canadian military circles. If a man was to risk his life for his country, he needed to know what his country was and have some feeling for it. As early as the North-West Rebellion and the Anglo-Boer War, the Canadian armed forces provided for "sketchers," military correspondents and on occasion an official military photographer. During the First World War we saw artists appointed, archives preserved, trophies and souvenirs collected, and official historians taken on strength. The importance of music and theatre was recognized early, not only in relieving the tedium of military routine but in promoting a corporate spirit and a sense of pride, and in fostering cheerful relations between garrisons and civilian populations. For years the Department of National Defence was alone among federal departments in developing a conscious, consistent and imaginative cultural policy and providing the funds to make it work.[24]

But perhaps the reluctance of Canadian governments to follow this lead and support culture showed a certain rough-hewn prudence. Culture in the larger perspective does create a sense of community, forming

41

common views of reality with which citizens can identify; but in detail, the commitment of art and artists may be to disrupt the existing order. As Rigaud elegantly puts it: "Culture is both the expression of collective certainties and the denial of those certainties."[25] In a fascinating section on intellectuals in his classical analysis of *Capitalism, Socialism and Democracy*, Joseph A. Schumpeter argues that the deeper motives of this section of the community tend to be hostile to capitalism.[26] Artists are not necessarily intellectuals but they generally share with them a critical view of society. Even in the nineteenth century support of culture could have meant subsidizing critics of the existing social order. This would have been as distasteful to liberal opinion (being a form of bribery) as to authoritarians. In Canada at this time few but governors general had the confidence of aristocrats in their own taste. Nor were many capitalists eager to take over art patronage. They lacked the fervid belief in private enterprise and the tax incentives that drove their American counterparts to bespeak monuments to its pride and power. If some of them were community leaders in the fostering of culture, they were modest ones compared to the American princes of commerce and industry who established the great foundations of Ford, Rockefeller, Guggenheim, Mellon, Frick and Carnegie, and lavished the ivy league universities, and the United States' libraries and galleries with endowments.

In 1932 the Miers Markham Report of the Museums Association of Great Britain noted that, while the Canadian federal treasury did support the Public Archives, the Historic Sites and Monuments Board, the National Parks Board and the War Museum and other Canadian institutions of the kind, "less is spent on the whole group of 125 institutions than is spent upon one of the great museums of Great Britain, Germany or the United States."[27]

42

It was the advent of radio that gradually opened official eyes to the importance of culture in the nation's life, to the dangers of continentalism and to the potential jurisdictional conflict between the federal government and the provinces over such matters. Canadians were already recognized as taking a leading role in the development and use of new electronic technologies: as early as 1907 Canada was named to the Administrative Council of the International Telegraphic Union in Geneva. Guglielmo Marconi's experiments with radio-telegraphy in Canada were helped forward by a subsidy of $80,000 from the federal treasury. But, again, there was no thought of a cultural dimension to this new invention until its use for broadcasting rather suddenly emerged after the First World War.

The Canadian Marconi Company in Montreal sold radio-telephone equipment to amateurs. A Marconi salesman called Max Smith thought it would be a good idea to promote his product by demonstrating it. Thus, in 1920 the Marconi Company's station with the call letters XWA became the first in Canada to begin regular broadcasts of records, news items and weather reports. As broadcaster, director, announcer and operator, Max Smith was Canada's first professional in radio.

Radio broadcasting began in England and the United States in the same year with a minimum of regulation. Such regulation as there was in Canada was taken care of by the Department of Public Works from 1900 until the Marine and Fisheries Department took over in 1909. The Naval Service administered it until it returned to Marine and Fisheries in 1922. It was the story of the National Gallery all over again.

In its first decade in Canada, radio was privately owned and supported by advertising. Except in Québec, which was poorly served because XWA was broadcasting only in English and the classical education of many

French speakers had not prepared them for the new technology, private stations proliferated throughout the country. All was confusion and Babel and many Canadians, painfully aware that there were no boundaries to the ether, began to feel threatened by the dominance of American commercial broadcasting.

Canadian National Railways, a Crown corporation which was already in the telegraph business, made an early move to meet the threat. Its president, Sir Henry Thornton, "saw radio as a great unifying force in Canada; to him the political concept transcended the commercial, and he set out consciously to create a sense of nationhood through the medium." So writes Frank Peers in *The Politics of Canadian Broadcasting, 1920-1951*.[28] Starting with a parlour-car service to entertain passengers, the first CNR radio station was opened in Ottawa in December 1924, to be followed by the creation of a national network. The first coast-to-coast hook-up was achieved on July 1, 1927, as part of the celebrations of the Diamond Jubilee of Confederation. Despite these efforts, Canadian radio stations were increasingly becoming affiliated to the new American networks and Canadian listeners were becoming addicted to American programming; in 1925 the Toronto *Telegram* ran a "radio popularity ballot" which gave the top seventeen places to American stations.

The Radio Act of 1927 established the Federal Radio Commission, and in the following year the government appointed a Royal Commission under the chairmanship of Sir John Aird, a Toronto banker, to consider the many questions that the Radio Act left unanswered. Who should pay for broadcasting? Should the air be used only for entertainment or only for education, or a combination of both? And who was to make the choice?

Although the constituting order-in-council noted that large numbers of Canadians preferred American

44

broadcasting, the Aird Commission, impressed by the British Broadcasting Corporation established by Royal Charter in 1923, took the view that "Canadian listeners want Canadian broadcasting," and concluded that their interests and those of the Canadian nation could be adequately served only by some form of public ownership, operation and control "behind which is the national power and prestige of the whole public of the Dominion of Canada."[29] But the real driving force in that direction – supported by the leaders of both the Liberal and Conservative parties – came from the Canadian Radio League. Founded in 1930 by Graham Spry and Alan Plaunt, the activists of the League included such figures as Brooke Claxton, R. K. Finlayson of Winnipeg and Norman Smith of Calgary; by the end of 1931, the League had recruited support from across the country among politicians of all parties, educational and church leaders, trade unions, women's organizations, farm organizations, the Canadian Legion, the business and financial community, and most of the press. Support came from both language groups, a consensus seldom achieved.

The government's tardiness in taking action, in the face of this clear lead from public opinion, was in part due to uncertainty about the constitutional legality of the Radio Telegraph Act of 1927, enacted to implement Canada's signature of the International Radio Telegraph Convention. On its referral to the Supreme Court of Canada, the Act was upheld by a majority of three to two. Québec, which had adopted its own Broadcasting Act and took the view that it alone could produce programs suited to the taste and mentality of the Québec people, appealed to the Judicial Committee of the Privy Council, with the support of Ontario. This appeal was lost. In upholding the right of the federal government to legislate in this area, their lordships observed, among

45

other things: "A divided control between transmitter and receiver could only lead to confusion and inefficiency."[30]

That the issue was primarily cultural was demonstrated vividly during the four-year life of the Canadian Radio Broadcasting Commission, the CBC's precursor. Attempting French programming as part of its service to the western provinces, the CRBC met with so much opposition that it began to arrange separate programming for Québec. The CBC continued this policy, so that the grand plan for national unity through radio only contributed further to creating a deeper cultural gulf between the two main language groups.

The CBC was established as a Crown corporation "to develop a national broadcasting service for all Canadians in both official languages which would be primarily Canadian in content and character."[31] Funds were to come from Parliament but the Corporation was independent, there was to be no political meddling with its administration. An attempt by C. D. Howe in its early days to restrict its activity to programming met with spirited resistance from Leonard Brockington, its first president, and was overruled in Cabinet.

There was controversy from time to time about the way the CBC was run. But it did use public funds in a way that provided a living for a number of Canadian writers, composers, performers and musicians; it did offer a forum for national conversation of a kind. In the early days of radio the CBC was a source of pride to Canadians: that is to say, programming in English pleased English-speakers, programming in French pleased French-speakers. The public sensed they owned an institution which its southern neighbour could not better.

The National Film Board, unlike the CBC subject to the direction and control of a cabinet minister, was established in 1939. Under John Grierson, "the father of us all," as film critic Martin Knelman has described him,

46

its wartime documentary films showed that in this art Canadians were pre-eminent in the world.[32] The Board also provided a base for other kinds of Canadian film production. Private film production in Québec, despite the language protection against American movies, barely developed, but the French-language films produced by the National Film Board reached a high standard. The Board's French-language section, indeed, took off on its own, making feature films while the English-language section was restricted to documentaries. The two sections existed side by side, as in the CBC, with little interaction.

The 1930s and 1940s also saw the birth of a number of national voluntary agencies and societies concerned with culture. The Canadian Historical Association, an outgrowth of the Historic Sites and Monuments Board of Canada (founded in 1919 chiefly by pressure from the Royal Society) had been set up in 1922 and was soon followed by the formation of the Royal Canadian Geographical Society (1929), the Canadian Political Science Association (1929), the Canadian Psychological Association (1939) and the Canadian Conference of the Arts (1945). Economists and sociologists were quick to leave their original home in the political science group to establish their own separate associations. The Canadian Library Association was founded in 1946 followed by the Canadian Humanities Association in 1948. Specialized groups in English, French, philosophy and other disciplines followed. The Dominion Drama Festival (founded, again, with the help of a governor general) began sponsoring playwriting competitions in 1932.[33] The Sculptors' Society of Canada and the Canadian Society of Graphic Art were established in 1932 and 1933 respectively. In 1936 the Société des écrivains canadiens was launched following the example of the Canadian Authors' Association (1921). The Canadian Writers' Foundation was set up to find money for writers in 1945; how great their need was may be inferred from the fact that in 1947 only 37 works of fiction were published in Canada, compared with 1,723 in Britain and 1,307 in the United States. In 1948 only 14 works of fiction were published in Canada, and six general books.[34]

It was time to stop making excuses for the absence of cultural policy, blaming it on commerce (as Samuel Butler had done) or on the hardships of pioneering (as many Canadians still do, despite the exploration literature of our heroic age). In circumstances that I shall return to, the federal government appointed a Royal Commission to investigate the subject on April 8, 1949.

The government had perceived that the arts should be encouraged; the people needed little persuasion. In Québec, where a new, highly educated and self-confident generation had come to recognize the devastation wrought upon their language and the arts by lack of private and public patronage, the forces of modernization were bringing about not only the Quiet Revolution but a far-reaching cultural revolution. In the whole of Canada television and newer technologies were about to change human consciousness.

The Royal Commission was appointed just before these momentous changes. The seeds of policy were there, the habits and style of movement well-rooted, and the directions, however dimly, perceived. But consciousness of the need to connect government and cultural policy, to connect the emerging cultures with one another, was still absent. The Commission was the first big chance.

*All we have to do is, each for himself, to keep down dissensions
which can only weaken, impoverish and keep back the country;
each for himself do all he can to increase its wealth, its strength
and its reputation; each for himself . . . to welcome every talent, to
hail every invention, to cherish every gem of art, to foster every
gleam of authorship, to honour every acquirement and every gift,
to lift ourselves to the level of our destinies. . . .*
                                        Thomas D'Arcy McGee, 1862.

*The statement that has been made so often that this is a con-
quered country is à propos de rien. Whether it was conquered or
ceded, we have a constitution now under which all British subjects
are in a position of absolute equality.*
                                        Sir John A. Macdonald, 1890.

*I am a subject of the British Crown but whenever I have to choose
between the interests of England and Canada it is manifest to me
that the interests of my country are identical with those of the
United States of America.*
                                        Sir Wilfrid Laurier, 1891.

*How utterly destitute of all light and charm are the intellectual
conditions of our people and the institutions of our public life!
How barren! How barbarous!*
                                        Archibald Lampman, 1892.

*The way to get things out of a government is to back them to the
wall, put your hands to their throats, and you will get all they
have.*
                                        Agnes Macphail, 1927.

*Civilization is a legacy of beliefs, of customs, of knowledge, slowly
acquired over the centuries, often difficult to justify through reason but which in turn are proven right like paths leading somewhere, as they open up to man his inner space.*
                                        A. de Saint-Exupéry, 1942.

Don't retire. Wait until you're dead.
                                        Sir James Dunn.

THREE

In the first chapter of this essay I tried to show that there are good reasons why governments all over the world should concern themselves with culture and especially why the federal government of Canada has a clear responsibility to foster it as a source of national integrity. Despite a fragmented educational system in which solutions of pluralism within the provinces ranged from out-and-out sectarianism to a thorough-going secularism, by the end of the Second World War Canadians had developed certain mental habits of interdependence based on the nature of our history and geography. These habits might be described as an agreement to differ. In the years between the wars this agreement was threatened by the powerful influence of privately financed American mass culture, which was perceived as a threat by Canadians of both languages and in all regions.

At the same time, cultural development was neglected and the two main language groups allowed to drift within their solitudes; except in the armed forces, assisted by the demands of war itself, there was no comprehensive policy and rationale in such cultural husbandry as was undertaken, even when it was handed over to Crown corporations. The cultural consequences of political acts in Canada were unforeseen and unexplored; communication systems designed to bind the country together instead divided it because of this unconsciousness and neglect of cultural effects. Government action in the cultural sector consisted of short-sighted responses to initiatives from voluntary societies, and depended on the energies of the determined few. No genuinely concerted effort was made by government to try to reconcile the increasing strains upon the mosaic of conflicting religions, nationalities and cultural attitudes that coloured the face of the land. The sense of nationality for which Canadians had fought and died in two world wars was allowed to fade among the jockeying of jurisdictions.

Meanwhile in Québec, cultural concerns began to return to the foreground of politics. Henri Bourassa, a convinced federalist, saw the importance of biculturalism as early as 1905. His nationalism was rooted in traditional Catholicism. A later generation preferred the nationalism of the historian Canon Lionel Groulx, who advocated a distinct Laurentian state as the best safeguard for French-Canadian culture within an adjusted Confederation.[1] These historical streams of thinking about the place of Québec culture in the world were to flow continually and with increasing turbulence into the present. Common to each was the conviction of the centrality of culture to the integrity and survival of the francophone community in North America.

Yet Canada as a whole emerged from the Second World War with a new sense of independence and confidence. The Canadian people, including Québécois, had poured out blood and treasure in distant places in defence, so their leaders told them, of spiritual and moral values. It was not altogether clear what these spiritual

52

and moral values might be or how they were to be nourished in peacetime. Canadians knew only that mature and civilized nations in Europe like Germany and Italy had gone berserk, freaked out on the mind-rotting acids of chauvinism, and that Canada along with her allies had succeeded in destroying the mad regimes. In the heart-searching that followed the humiliations of Hong Kong and Dieppe, Canadians had begun to find the springs of their own strength. They had come through it all to win the flowers and kisses of victory, not as conquerors but as liberators. They had been somewhere important before their southern neighbour; they had played a generous part in world history. The fever chart of their ordeal is to be found in poems like Douglas Le Pan's "The Net and the Sword"; such works could persuade Canadians that they shared in the dignity of mankind.

The 1930s and 1940s had been a period of beginnings and stirrings attesting to the growing awareness of cultural needs. Conflicting "movements" emerged. The war and its aftermath both stimulated a new nationalism and brought in new influences from abroad. All branches of the arts were affected and nowhere more clearly than in Montréal. There, the Contemporary Arts Society had been founded in 1939 by the painter John Lyman. With the fall of Paris in 1940, French intellectuals, writers and artists arrived as refugees and introduced the new contemporary movements in art and architecture from Europe. Alfred Pellan, a Canadian and a Québécois, was among those who had returned from Paris and he soon became a leader amongst the artists. Goodridge Roberts, Paul-Emile Borduas, Jacques de Tonnancour, Jean-Paul Riopelle and others began to make their mark at this time. Similar developments were occurring in Toronto and in the West. Perhaps the most important event of those years, considering what it led to, was a conference in Kingston in 1941 organized on behalf of the Royal Canadian Academy by André Bieler, artist-in-residence at Queen's University. The outcome was the inauguration of the Federation of Canadian Artists, led by sculptor Elizabeth Wyn Wood and painter Lawren Harris. The Federation was to lead the first concerted approach to the federal government for support of the arts. It had been inspired by the work in Britain of the Council for the Encouragement of Music and the Arts, a body led by John Maynard Keynes which in 1945 became the Arts Council of Great Britain.[2]

The opportunity for an approach to government came in June 1944 when the House of Commons, looking to the restoration of peace, set up a Special Committee on Reconstruction and Re-establishment, which came to be known as the Turgeon Committee. Several voluntary societies immediately set about preparing memoranda, and then someone had the bright idea of getting together and submitting a concerted brief and delivering it in person to the Turgeon Committee. The result was the famous "March on Ottawa" (in fact, most of the marchers came by bus from Toronto) by three distinct groups acting together. The first represented the Canadian Federation of Artists and the Royal Canadian Academy. The second was a consortium of four painting societies (Water Colour, Canadian Group, Graphic Arts, and Painter-Etchers and Engravers), the Royal Architectural Institute, the Canadian Society of Landscape Artists and Town Planners, the Sculptors' Society, the Canadian Authors' Association, the Dominion Drama Festival, the Canadian Guild of Potters, and a music committee headed by Sir Ernest MacMillan. The third group was a deputation of three reluctantly nominated members of the Toronto Arts and Letters Club. The brief was endorsed by the Société des écrivains canadiens.

The brief to the Turgeon Committee pointed out

that in Canada there were millions who had never seen an original work of art, or attended a symphony concert or a professionally produced play, while in the largest cities thousands of professional artists faced a field so limited as to force them into activities unsuited to their talents. Cultural resources, the brief continued, should be more actively developed to improve the international image of Canada while giving greater security to artists and a richer and happier life for Canadians generally. The chief recommendations were to establish a government body, preferably a non-political board, to promote a national cultural program of support for music, drama, film, and the visual and literary arts; to provide community centres for artistic activities; to promote Canadian art abroad; to improve copyright protection for artists; to improve industrial design, housing and town planning; and to establish an orchestral training centre and a national library. The Turgeon Committee was evidently impressed and recommended that the government set up either a department of cultural affairs or a non-political board.[3]

There is no evidence that any large body of citizens was shocked by this suggestion. They had not been shocked when the CNR, in the days before public broadcasting, had spent public money to put on radio dramas celebrating Canadian history. Or, before the CBC was set up, by the weekly broadcast in Québec of a program paid for by the provincial government, "L'Heure provinciale."

"At every critical juncture of our national life," the historian A. R. M. Lower was to recall later, "when we have been faced with a choice between individualism and socialization, we have chosen socialization." This was another cultural habit of Canadians that was to determine the approach to cultural questions. It was Lower's view that some communities grow, while others are made: "Canada is one that has been made, a country of a plan."[4] But the comparative inertness of private enterprise in Canada probably had its roots in the small scale and limited power of Canadian corporations compared with their United States counterparts.

The experiment in collaboration between arts groups inspired the establishing of other similar bodies, such as the Canadian Museums Association in 1946. In the same year the music committee under Sir Ernest MacMillan formed the Canadian Music Council. And on December 5, 1945, sixteen organizations combined to form the Canadian Arts Council under the chairmanship of Herman Voaden. The body began its life in Montréal where it had the vigorous support of Jean Bruchési, founder of the Société des écrivains, and Roland Charlebois, director of L'Ecole des Beaux Arts; its activities were to include membership of the Canadian delegation to the first General Assembly of UNESCO in 1946. French- and English-speaking intellectuals and artists found little difficulty in co-operating in a common cultural cause.

The recommendations of the Turgeon Committee became the seed of the Royal Commission on the Arts, Letters and Sciences, chaired by Vincent Massey, which was appointed on April 8, 1949. The Report of the Massey Commission has come to be regarded as the cornerstone for much that has followed in the development of Canadian cultural policy and institutions.

The political origins of this turning point in Canadian cultural history are worth investigating. According to J. W. Pickersgill's book *My Years with St. Laurent*, the first suggestion for a commission on the arts had been made at the National Liberal Convention in August 1948 by the Canadian University Liberal Federation. Brooke Claxton learned that Liberal students were "bitterly disappointed" when the suggestion had not been supported by the Convention. Pickersgill says that in a memorandum to Prime Minister Mackenzie King on September 29, 1948, Claxton enclosed draft terms of reference for a commission which he suggested should be headed by Vincent Massey.[5] Efforts to trace this memorandum of Claxton's have so far been unsuccessful, but there seems no reason to doubt its existence.

As for King's reaction, Pickersgill remarks, "I knew that the very idea of such a commission would have been rejected by Mackenzie King as ridiculous." King's ideas about what was ridiculous were not those of other men. That he cared about the trophies of history we know, since he went to the trouble of building a ruin in the vicinity of Ottawa, made up of stones carried away from ancient and hallowed edifices in Europe. Massey in his memoirs records, with some irritation, that King once put the Canadian High Commission in London to the pains of begging a few bits of rubble from the wreckage of the bombed Mother of Parliaments and sending them to Canada.

In any case, King was aware of the cultural community's demands for government action to assist the arts. On April 16, 1946, he received a lucid and forceful statement of the Canadian Arts Council's case from its president, Herman Voaden. Reiterating the Council's proposals made to the Turgeon Committee in 1944, Voaden cited their favourable reception by members of all parties, by the press and by the public. In a passage that seems to foreshadow Secretary of State Pelletier's policies of democratization twenty years later, Voaden wrote of the need "to serve the entire nation – especially smaller cities, towns, villages and rural areas, and frontier districts." The Canadian Arts Council thought the federal government should set aside $10 million to encourage the provinces to build community centres. A National Arts Board could also provide cultural information and services to UNESCO. Voaden wanted to meet with officials of at least four government departments: External Affairs (because of the international implications); Trade and Commerce (because of the need to improve industrial design); Secretary of State ("because the arts are important in achieving a common citizenship"); and Health and Welfare (concerned with community planning and recreation).[6]

In forwarding this interesting letter to the Prime Minister, the Secretary of the Cabinet, R. Gordon Robertson noted, "The Council mentioned the Department of External Affairs but it is difficult to see how the Department is concerned in the matter."[7] From the perspective of history, it is not difficult to see why External Affairs should have been interested. If there was a reason to recommend their exclusion from the cultural area, Robertson does not remember it. And in the event it did not matter, since King was, in any case, too busy to meet with the Arts Council. He was, after all, preoccupied with higher matters of state like getting his Order of Merit from the Queen, and maybe one for Pat II, his dog.

If Pickersgill is right, at least two men in External Affairs, Vincent Massey and Lester B. Pearson, were exceedingly interested in the idea of a royal commission on the arts. "Claxton had discussed the idea with me," Pickersgill writes, "and I in turn had discussed it with Pearson before St. Laurent became Prime Minister. In a message Pearson sent me from Paris on 5 November 1948, he said he had seen Massey in London and advised him not to take on any other task until he had seen St. Laurent. Pearson added, 'the Royal Commission idea which you mentioned seemed to me to be an imaginative and excellent one and Massey would, of course, be admirable for that work.'"

Pickersgill believes St. Laurent was persuaded by Pearson and Claxton that a commission on the arts would be in the public interest "as well as being good

58

politics." What appealed to St. Laurent, by this account, was the chance to deal with broadcasting and the universities. (Like Claxton he had been involved actively in the Radio League of Canada, although he once confessed to Pickersgill that he was not very enthusiastic about subsidizing ballet dancing.)[8]

The universities, by 1948, were approaching a crisis. Federal grants to veteran students under the Veterans' Rehabilitation Act would soon be drying up, and in Québec especially, where Premier Duplessis, typically, was ignoring the increasing demands of higher education, something would have to be done.

When the Royal Commission on National Development in the Arts, Letters and Sciences was created in 1949 no one was surprised that Vincent Massey was appointed chairman. He was patently the right choice.

Outside the Department of National Defence, no group of Canadians was more aware of the relevance of the arts to national life than the working diplomats of External Affairs. In a time when cables, telephones and transatlantic planes had narrowed the scope of their initiative, one of the subjects of diplomacy that held interest for cultivated envoys was culture. Canadian diplomats were also aware that the status of their country had changed. Canada was at the height of its power and prestige, taking an honourable place at the council tables of the world. At the dinner tables, too, Canada felt the need to acquire civilized graces.

Vincent Massey possessed them. What was more, as High Commissioner in London, he had come through air raids and had seen at first hand the importance of culture to a nation fighting for its life. As a private citizen he had been active in the foundation bequeathed by his grandfather Hart Massey to give his native Toronto a concert hall, a cultural centre for students, and other cultural benefactions. A connoisseur of art, litera-

59

ture and theatre, he had contributed his acumen and taste to the British National Gallery as well as an important art collection to the National Gallery of Canada.

The terms of the order-in-council setting up the Massey Commission, drafted under the eye of St. Laurent, echo the language of Sir Henry Thornton and the Radio League: "It is in the national interest to give encouragement to institutions which express national feeling, promote common understanding and add to the richness and variety of Canadian life, rural as well as urban." Perhaps in that last phrase there is a sense of the dilemma of all agricultural countries undergoing modernization – what Marx called "the idiocy of rural life."

St. Laurent was anxious to avoid conflict with Québec over education, a provincial preserve. Thus it was essential to make the right choice of a French-Canadian commissioner. There was no doubt in anyone's mind that Father Lévesque was the man. The Most Reverend Georges-Henri Lévesque, a Dominican who was Dean of social sciences at Laval University, was one of the moving forces in Québec's cultural revolution and a committed federalist. Possessed of tact and subtlety, he was a genial representative of French-Canadian culture, a spirit powerful and clear. It was he who found the Massey Report its epigraph in the writings of St. Augustine, a definition of nationhood to set beside Vico's: "A nation is an association of reasonable beings united in a peaceful sharing of the things they cherish, therefore to determine the quality of a nation, you must consider what those things are."[9] Some "reasonable beings" in Québec were to assail Father Lévesque bitterly for accepting appointment to a federal royal commission on national culture. As St. Laurent had foreseen, there were fears that the federal government was clearing the way for the invasion of provincial rights.

The other commissioners were Arthur Surveyer, a

Montréal civil engineer chosen for his technical knowledge of the hardware of broadcasting; Dr. Norman A. M. MacKenzie, president of the University of British Columbia and past president of the University of New Brunswick, who had a broad knowledge of educational interests in both the Atlantic and the Pacific regions; and Dr. Hilda Neatby, professor of history at the University of Saskatchewan.[10] There were no artists, poets or musicians on the Commission.

The commissioners were squarely representative of traditional culture. But in 1949 teenagers had not yet come into enough money to create monuments to their own taste; the Beat generation had not yet surfaced, let alone the Beatles; and there was no reason for the Massey Commission to perplex itself with attempts to distinguish high from pop culture. The cult of jazz was well advanced but the commissioners were not the kind of people to notice it. Broadcasting, while well established, was, technologically speaking, in its infancy.

Television would soon begin to transform culture and human consciousness in Canada as elsewhere. In reaction to its pressures for cultural uniformity, regional and minority cultures all over the world began to reassert themselves. The nationalisms which had become discredited in two world wars were to return in new forms, accompanied in some countries – and even in Canada – by violence. In an age when a single urban guerrilla could carry more fire-power than a regiment on the field of Waterloo, the nationalism of the smallest minority could become a force to reckon with.

The Massey Commission was to examine and make recommendations on the principles that should govern national policy in respect of radio, then in its heyday, and television, which was not yet launched in Canada; inquire into the scattered federal cultural agencies already in existence and comment on their scope,

61

activities and future development; suggest ways for Canada to relate to international bodies such as UNESCO; and study the processes responsible for starting the few cultural agencies in existence and their relationships.

"Our concern throughout," they were to report in 1951, "was with the needs and desires of the citizens in relation to science, literature, art, music, the drama, broadcasting.... We found it necessary to attempt a general survey of the arts, letters and sciences in Canada."[11] In this survey, 462 briefs were submitted to the Commission by 13 federal agencies, 7 provincial governments (Québec was not one of them), 87 national organizations, 262 local bodies (including many from Québec), 32 commercial radio stations, and scores of private individuals. In addition, special studies were commissioned on 40 specific topics and more than 1,200 witnesses were heard in the course of 224 meetings and 10,000 miles of travel across Canada.

So ambitious a government investigation had never before been undertaken. As a post-graduate student in England at the time, I remember often being asked by fellow students from Britain, the United States and France why any country would wish to examine its culture so closely and critically. At home in Canada, the postwar economic and social policies of the federal government that would influence the security and stability of the nation for a generation were being determined after all in secret behind baize doors by a handful of bureaucrats and academics. Had the subject of culture become more important than that of the economy or just politically less dangerous?

The report, tabled on June 1, 1951, was on a scale proportionate to the Commission's lofty terms of reference: 200,000 words accompanied by a volume of special studies, in effect a massive stocktaking of the intangibles contributing to Canadian tradition and identity and shaping Canada for the future. The word culture was sedulously avoided and a conscious effort made to adopt a tone that was plain-spoken rather than high-falutin'. The Prime Minister carried the report into the House of Commons, as it were, with tongs. He was careful to say no one in the government had read it. But within eighteen days he took the necessary steps to present legislation recommending grants to the universities. Even Maurice Duplessis would, at first, accept the extra funds for education, though he later rejected them as encroachments on provincial jurisdiction.

On page 5, the Massey Report confronts the question of what business the government has with the arts: "In most modern states there are ministries of 'fine arts' or of 'cultural affairs.' Some measure of official responsibility is now accepted in all civilized countries whatever political philosophy may prevail."[12] Perhaps it is a somewhat evasive statement, an argument *e consentu gentium* of the kind one falls back on in the presence of known philistines. It should be remembered that this was the era of the cold war, when McCarthyism in the United States was to make its most damaging effect in the cultural arena.

The style of the report was academic in the best sense. According to Father Lévesque, the "soul" of the document is to be found in Chapter 14 on the Scholar and the Scientist, where the prose becomes fluent and eloquent. The sections on the arts themselves were more scrappy, as though the commissioners were less sure of their ground. The paragraphs on literature and writing in general can only be described as depressing. Nevertheless, this highly effective document was to become a watershed in Canadian cultural policy. Almost all its recommendations were eventually implemented in some fashion or other. Before it, everything was tentative, incoherent, a patchwork of band-aid remedies – though a patchwork in which the historical eye could perceive a distinctively Canadian pattern. After the Massey Report, Canadian governments, provincial as well as federal, began to be drawn reluctantly toward the need to develop cultural policy more consciously and to try and avoid the patchwork of the past.

Considering its weight and complexity, the Massey Report's initial reception by the press was understandably cautious. Its recommendations were numerous and seemed bold, proposing far-reaching changes in the relationship of government to culture. Yet there was nothing revolutionary about it. One might even ask whether it did not kick down a door that was already open. The urban middle class, with their increasing wealth, leisure and education, were probably ahead of the commissioners, and almost certainly ahead of the government and the media. The initiative, after all, for what was to become a famous Shakespeare festival came from small-town businessmen in Ontario.

The fearfulness with which governments in Canada have approached culture, though indicative of the narrow horizons of the power holders, is itself evidence of the subject's growing importance. "La phobie de l'intervention fédérale," Jean Chauvin was to reflect a year after the Massey Report was tabled, "voire sur le plan culturel, dans le domaine des arts, des lettres et des sciences, vient de notre faiblesse et de notre crainte de tout contact étranger." In his initial acceptance of federal grants for higher education, Premier Maurice Duplessis was in Chauvin's opinion "plus intelligent et réaliste que ses scribes."[13]

The day after St. Laurent tabled the Massey Report, the Winnipeg *Free Press* commented: "It is a reflection of the instinctive opposition of Canadians against state domination in these fields that the Massey Report proposes a minimum of new government machinery to

64

carry out its proposals. There is no commissar of culture, no minister of fine arts and propaganda, in the recommendations of the Massey Commission. A new body to be known as the Canada Council is recommended." Noting that this might turn out to be the most important single recommendation in the report, the *Free Press* went on to say, "Such a Council would presumably enable Canadians to help themselves."[14]

The report came down strongly in favour of public ownership and control of broadcasting, with A. Surveyer dissenting from his colleagues' view that broadcasting was a public service and not a business opportunity.

The proposal that the state go into art patronage in a big way made many editorial writers uneasy. They felt that one could not buy culture; it was something that had to grow by itself. It was not widely understood that the National Gallery, for example, under Eric Brown had already begun to play an important part in the development of Canadian art by choosing to purchase works by some Canadian painters and not others.

Editorial writers may have been victims of romantic delusions about how artists and writers should live. According to these ideas they should starve in attics or log cabins, be ignored during their lives, and recognized only after they have died of drink or venereal disease or tuberculosis. Newspapermen and their publishers are especially addicted to this view of the artist's lot, since they sometimes fear they themselves have sold out to avoid it. On this point Jacques Rigaud contributes his enlightened common sense: "Sufficient it is for the artist to struggle with himself."[15] In 1951, anyway, many of the intelligentsia assumed that the people at large were too crass to fork over tax dollars to a bunch of wild-eyed painters, hairy poets and junky musicians, let alone to buy Rembrandts and Picassos for aesthetes or provide symphonies at a discount to stuffed shirts. The view lingers on to this day in the guise of a false populism, whose logic would exclude expenditure on higher education unless it were totally vocational.

St. Laurent's government took its time about implementing the Massey proposal of a Canada Council sacred to the Muses. Father Lévesque recalls that when Vincent Massey became Governor General in 1952 he felt it would be improper for him to go on pressing for action on the Commission's recommendations. He passed the torch to Lévesque.

According to Father Lévesque, his friend St. Laurent told him that the obstacle to action was C. D. Howe, the Liberal minister who was widely believed to be the embodiment of business efficiency and common sense. Howe had tried to clip the wings of the infant CBC. But we have already seen that the real princes of Canadian industry and finance – men like Sir Edmund Walker, Sir Henry Thornton and Sir John Aird, like the real princes of Québec intellectual life – had possessed the vision to see that public support of culture was vital to Canada's survival. No doubt Howe was not the only cabinet member who thought the arts too airy-fairy a proposition for public funding. Five years passed without any action by the government.

Lévesque knew that St. Laurent was worried about fiscal relations with the province of Québec, but felt that the Prime Minister could be won over if Howe's objections were overcome. In a 1977 radio broadcast on the origins of the Canada Council, Father Lévesque said, "But Mr. Massey – he wanted that Council!" At a dinner at Rideau Hall in 1956, Massey saw to it that Father Lévesque sat next to C. D. Howe. "Is it true, Mr. Howe," the wily Dominican asked, "that you are preparing a prototype warplane at a cost of $100 million?" Howe admitted it. Lévesque reminded him that in the recent war Canada had fought to defend Christian spiritual and cultural values. But in peacetime we were not ready to spend $100 million to support them. Howe laughed. "What a good politician you would have been!" he said.

Maurice Lamontagne, a protégé of Lévesque's who at this time was the Prime Minister's economic adviser, recalls that in July 1956 Louis St. Laurent was at a loss what to say in a speech he was to give at a meeting representing the universities – a speech Lamontagne would have to draft. There was a crisis in educational funding. Lamontagne suggested that he announce plans to launch the Canada Council. "You have the money there," he added. Two immensely rich tycoons had died (Isaak Walton Killam and Sir James Hamet Dunn) leaving large fortunes that provided a $100 million bonanza in succession duties. St. Laurent smiled. "I will speak to Howe," he said. At about 6 p.m. the same day the Prime Minister telephoned Lamontagne and said, "It's all right. Prepare my speech for November and start work on the legislation."

J. W. Pickersgill added his recollection of the events in the same broadcast. He had been in the habit of walking to work, he said. One morning in the summer of 1956 he was walking along Mariposa, an important street in the affluent village of Rockcliffe on the edge of Ottawa. There, he encountered Dr. John Deutsch also on his way to work. Deutsch was at that time a mandarin in the federal administration, and was to become one of the nation's wisest advisers to both levels of government. A westerner of great common sense, he hated any kind of waste. And he was capable of the long view. As the two were passing Ashbury College, Deutsch raised the subject of the estates, saying in his quiet, thoughtful manner, "Here are these two millionaires who have died and there is going to be about $50 million in succession duties come from each of them, which is a kind of windfall. It just seems a shame to piddle it away on ordinary govern-

67

ment expenditure. Something special ought to be done with it."

John Deutsch was as interested in education and the civilizing role of government as he was in finance and economics and he struck a responsive chord in talking to his friend. Pickersgill, so he reports, was seized with an idea. "Why shouldn't $50 million be used as a capital grant to universities and the other $50 million on the Canada Council?" He was so excited by this notion that he walked straight into the Prime Minister's office without even taking his coat off and announced the brainwave.[16]

In this way the government supposedly backed into its decision to give public support to the arts.

> And malt does more than Milton can
> To justify God's ways to man.[17]

On November 12, 1956, Prime Minister St. Laurent announced his decision to recommend the creation of the Canada Council to the next session of Parliament. The occasion was the National Conference on Higher Education in Ottawa. The Prime Minister reviewed the development of a national cultural policy in Canada and, citing legal precedents, asserted the right of the federal government to grant sums of money to individuals and organizations with such restrictions and conditions as Parliament might impose. He said:

> An extensive national cultural policy has been gradually developed ... although many Canadians may feel that, in certain sectors, it has been too modest and timid. ... This policy has been aimed at strengthening and developing our main cultures without attempting to impose either of them upon any Canadians. It is based upon the principle that

68

private initiative has the main responsibility in most aspects of our cultural development. It has provided financial assistance to individuals, voluntary organizations and institutions in order to support them without attempting, however, to control their activities. Finally this policy has also included the setting up of several public agencies which were deemed essential for the development and the adequate expression of our cultural life.

In a brief peroration modestly offered St. Laurent said:

I think you will agree that indeed, the world today needs abundant sources of intellectual and moral energies. Canada wants to be one of those sources, and it has already begun to be one of those sources in several international organizations. With that purpose in mind, we must further develop and enrich our own national soul.... [18]

Just as governors general have more than once provided the impetus for cultural development, prime ministers have been the politicians to speak for it – with rare exceptions. In the absence of a federal ministry of culture no other minister held responsibility in this area until quite recently, when it was assigned to the Secretary of State. When future generations come to assess St. Laurent's achievements during his years of comfortable power, the contents of this speech written by Lamontagne will rank high.

A measure for the establishment of the Canada Council was announced in the Speech from the Throne on January 8, and the Canada Council Act received Royal Assent on March 28, 1957. Introducing the bill, St. Laurent said that the Council would be continuing the work already being done by the universities and by such

69

voluntary bodies as the Royal Canadian Institute, L'Association canadienne-française pour l'avancement des sciences, the Royal Canadian Academy of the Arts, the Royal Society of Canada, the Canadian Writers' Foundation, the Canadian Social Science Research Council and the Humanities Association of Canada. (The Canada Council, in fact, retained the services of several of these voluntary bodies, and owed much of its early success to the energy, experience and wisdom of such men as Walter Herbert of the Canada Foundation, Dr. John E. Robbins of the Social Sciences and Humanities Research councils, and Arthur Gelber of the Canadian Conference of the Arts.) St. Laurent quoted the Massey Report to the effect that "we have not much right to be proud of our record as patrons of the arts." Canadian scholars and students as well as artists had relied too long on assistance from foreign sources, notably the great American trusts of Carnegie, Rockefeller and Ford, the Nuffield Foundation in Britain, and the munificence of foreign governments.[19]

The debate on the bill was not distinguished, though some members made interesting observations. T. S. Barnett, the CCF member for Comox-Alberni, remarked, "I have some conviction and some hope that in these areas the things which tend to unite us as Canadians run deeper than loyalty to the political expediency of any particular party in this country." And he reported a rare resolution by the Canadian Labour Congress commending the government for proposing the Canada Council and suggesting that a member of the Congress be appointed to the Council.

Some of the attitudes and anxieties of the members who spoke are worth glancing at. The expression "social sciences," oddly enough, alarmed some members, and not only because they had found it on the covers of the (social studies) texts brought home by their children.

Mr. Blackmore found the seeds of the Canada Council in a subversive conspiracy initiated by UNESCO; he saw it as an establishment "under which the children of Canada will be indoctrinated against God or the creation." Other debaters spoke of "state culture" and referred to Russia. It must be remembered that during this period in the United States, Senator McCarthy was conducting his campaign of smear and innuendo: in the hearings of the Senate Committee on Un-American Activities the careers of many writers and artists as well as public servants were ruined.

Deeper anxieties were expressed by members like Solon Low, the Social Credit leader, who saw cultural concerns as "frills – and that is what this is – a frill. . . . " These anxieties were based on the Puritan view that the arts were merely to be enjoyed and that enjoyment was somehow wicked – or at least something to be put off to the end of a day of hard work. And perhaps on the amoral behaviour of many artists. Even among those who supported the bill there was a feeling that only those works of art which carried moral uplift were to be cherished. Most discussion centred on the need to support universities. Several members warned that they were going to keep an eagle eye on the Canada Council.[20]

It had taken the government years, let us remember, to carry out the Massey Commission's major recommendation. Consciously or unconsciously, cabinet members tended to perceive culture as a disruptive force in the community, and they may have been right. In all societies the heralds of new views of reality are feared. Religion, for example, has often been born in the desert from which the prophets returned to human community with dire messages promising woe to the cities and destruction to the wicked and forward hearts in high places. Their violent imaginings were quickly contained and hedged in by priestly interpreters and institutions. In ancient Ireland, for example, the *fili*, the poets and seers, were themselves organized into the hierarchy of "men of art." Along with the judges and lawyers, or *brehons*, they were feared for their spiritual power.

On a more mundane level, the economist Joseph Schumpeter had foreseen the result of educating large numbers of citizens beyond their intellectual means, or at least above their station.

> All those who are unemployed or unsatisfactorily employed or unemployable drift into the vocations in which standards are least definite or in which aptitudes and acquirements of a different order count. They swell the host of intellectuals in the strict sense of the term whose numbers hence increase disproportionately. They enter it in a thoroughly discontented frame of mind. Discontent breeds resentment. And it often rationalizes itself into that social criticism which ... is in any case the intellectual spectator's typical attitude toward men, classes and institutions especially in a rationalist and utilitarian civilization.[21]

Such considerations may explain why Canadian governments have found it difficult to formulate a cultural policy, a difficulty reinforced by the liberal pluralist tradition of independence of the intellectual with its consequent reluctance to co-opt him. Government support might corrupt social critics. The United States has chosen its traditional free enterprise approach. Let the private sector (prodded by tax incentives) support culture. But in Canada the private sector, when given the opportunity to contribute, say, to the endowment fund of the Canada Council, or the trust funds of the National Museums, has taken little advantage of it (with a few commendable exceptions). Canadian governments for their part are not sure of their rights in the matter, or even of the efficacy

72

of federal financing of aspects of culture (with the exception of Québec), unlike the governments of other democracies or planned non-liberal societies. Canada is in some confusion in this as in other policy areas.

Looking back on the Massey Report, the historian A. R. M. Lower was to remark that the Commission was appointed in response "not to the personal desire of any one man, but to the feeling, to be sensed in a multitude of directions, that the time had come when the spirit of the Canadian community must find its voice." Lower saw the report as a defensive document:

> How can we maintain a Canadian community in any vital sense of the term against the unparalleled strength – in every aspect of life – of our great neighbour?... The Report of the Commission is a classic document. The Canadian state now turns to the highest function of a state, building the spiritual structure (the word is not used in the religious sense) of a civilization, the material foundations of which it has already sturdily laid. If the builders can continue to be men and women of the calibre and vision of those who prepared this Report, the work will go forward to brilliant achievement in future ages.[22]

In the late 1950s the whole of Canada was undergoing an acceleration of the process called modernization. The country's gross national product had grown from nearly $25,000 million in 1954 to over $31,000 million three years later. Spending on public libraries (to take just one example of cultural funding) had grown nearly sevenfold in the twenty years before the Canada Council was established. Modernization has been defined as including secularization, rationalization, bureaucratization, industrialization, urbanization, structural differentiation, consolidation of policy making, and the elimination of political and social inequalities.[23] The Canadian people were carried along on a tremendous surge in wealth and education, demonstrating a new interest in discovering and sharing their human resources. There was a sense of confidence and optimism in moulding one's future. With the advantage of hindsight one can see how symbolic was the euphoric Report of the Royal Commission on Canada's Economic Prospects, published in 1957. It was chaired by Walter Gordon, one of the country's leading nationalists, and written by Douglas Le Pan, who at that time was still a senior bureaucrat in Ottawa and had not yet decided to become teacher, poet and writer.

What was then known as automation of many industrial and business functions was believed to be bringing about an increase of leisure. The point was raised during the debate on the Canada Council bill. There were fears that without some enjoyable occupation, Satan would find mischief still for idle hands to do. Fears of technological unemployment were allayed by economic growth, which produced new jobs, mostly in service occupations. In any case, the need for culture was being widely discussed, though not often in the context of nation-building. The major urban centres saw cultural facilities as necessary to attract new industry, reflecting the growing sophistication of business executives and rising expectations of the labour force.

The Canada Council held its first meeting on April 30, 1957. "I remember that it was a perfectly beautiful day," Andrée Paradis, a Council member, was to recall in 1977. "The sun was shining all over Ottawa." The Council met in the Parliament Buildings. Mme Paradis recalls that for every member of the Council it was a day of hope.

As vice-chairman, Father Lévesque insisted on

74

making his opening address in French. This was something that the chairman, Brooke Claxton, had not envisaged, but finding that Lévesque was ready to resign on the issue, he agreed. It was the beginning of a deep and pleasant friendship between the two men. Claxton was new to the problems of bilingualism but he showed himself willing to learn. "I had to train him in that field," Lévesque recalled later. But Claxton was not new to the centrality of culture in building a sense of national purpose; he had been Minister of National Defence for eight years.

The policy of the Canada Council announced in 1962 by its second chairman, Dr. Claude Bissell, had in fact been pursued from the beginning: "We believe that our resources should go to the support of full-time professional artists and organizations that are likely to achieve some degree of national prominence and to efforts to create an audience for first class performance."[24] When the Council began its program of awarding grants to writers and artists and scholars to help them with their work, it might have been expected to be overwhelmed by requests for handouts for needy applicants. This did not happen. Indeed a number of artists and scholars had been making their way without help, many of them by leaving the country, like Raymond Massey, Paul-Emile Borduas, Jean-Paul Riopelle, Raoul Jobin, Joseph Plaskett, Mordecai Richler, Mavis Gallant and A. J. M. Smith. Others, like F. R. Scott, E. J. Pratt, Morley Callaghan, Hugh MacLennan, Yves Thériault, the Group of Seven, Jack Shadbolt, and Gordon Webber had stayed at home and managed nonetheless.

But as soon as the applications for help began to exceed by significant numbers the available awards, the Canada Council was seen as an organization for withholding money. There was always a demand for more, and as the years went by the Council was dismayed to find itself committed to a number of large-scale institutional pensioners, such as the National Ballet, major theatre groups and the symphony orchestra societies. The endowment fund had not been significantly increased by large benefactions from the private sector, and it became necessary to find new sources of income in the form of annual parliamentary votes.

In part because the Council concentrated on aid to professional scholars, artists and writers, several provinces began to fund amateur and recreational culture, though they were to do a great deal more than this. Some of their activities led to eventual conflict with the Canada Council over the amount of support given to non-professionals. But it should be noted that such conflicts merely underlined the early signs of confusion once interest in cultural development was seriously addressed. The need for a comprehensive policy to be developed by all interested jurisdictions was rarely raised, each interested group forgetful that the money, after all, comes from the pockets of the same taxpayers and the output of the artist is for everyone.

At the time of its appointment, though, the Council was given wide support for its attempts to raise the standards of Canadian achievement in the arts. We forget today how important this question of quality was in the 1950s. One example in 1956, the launching of a literary quarterly, *The Tamarack Review*, by a group of Toronto writers and editors, was inspired by the conviction that there was a need to cultivate excellence. This was equally true for Jean Gascon who founded le Théatre du Nouveau Monde in 1951. But perhaps the most apposite was the beginning of the Stratford Shakespearean Festival under Tyrone Guthrie in 1953. The success of the festival in its early years showed that Canadians would support arts of professional standard. And the Council's efforts, like those of the CBC before it, did help

76

to improve the quantity and quality of Canadian achievement, especially in literature, music and the performing arts.

It was beginning to look as if you could buy culture after all: bread and books went hand in hand. It was a time of extravagant hopes for what could be achieved by education, and the expansion of universities was beginning to establish new markets for culture. The new community centres across the country provided showcases and incentives to produce entertainments to fill them even if the "entertainments" were too often made in the United States.

And the lift to morale given by grants of public money to creative talent was almost as important as the money itself. Writers and artists began to form a habit of listing their Canada Council fellowships and grants in their publicity releases, since these amounted to a kind of endorsement by their peers. A vital part in mediating between administrators and artists was played by the late Peter Dwyer, a highly civilized man who directed the Council's arts programs in those years, and whose personal qualities won him the trust of writers and artists. His earlier career in British counter-intelligence had not dulled his wits nor his wit.[25]

The Massey Commission had been a creature of the idealism and economic power generated in Canada by the Second World War, but its recommendations crystalized a Canadian train of thought which had been developing since Confederation by fits and starts. This was the notion that, unlike its southern neighbour, the government of Canada had a part to play in fostering culture as it had in building roads, railways and communication systems. As yet, though, the *central* importance of this function to nation-building and public survival was hardly understood, at any rate in federal government circles. The same could not be said of Québec.

We have come to a period in the history of this young country where premature dissolution seems to be at hand. What will be the outcome? How long can the present fabric last? Can it last at all?
Sir Wilfrid Laurier, 1891.

Québec is the most interesting thing by much that I have seen on this continent.
Matthew Arnold, 1895.

There is Ontario patriotism, Québec patriotism, or Western patriotism, each based on the hope that it may swallow up the others, but there is no Canadian patriotism, and we can have no Canadian nation when we have no Canadian patriotism. The Nationalist movement in Québec is the greatest guarantee of the permanency of Canada.
Henri Bourassa, 1907.

Do you wish to know what public opinion is? It is the opinion of those who are against us.
Maurice Duplessis.

Not life, liberty, and the pursuit of happiness, but peace, order and good government are what the national government of Canada guarantees. . . . One of the blessings of Canadian life is that there is no Canadian way of life, much less two, but a unity under the Crown admitting of a thousand diversities.
W. L. Morton, 1961.

The desire not to be impinged upon, to be left to oneself has been a mark of high civilization that derives from a conception of freedom which, for all its religious roots, is scarcely older, in its developed state, than the Renaissance or the Reformation.
Isaiah Berlin, 1969.

FOUR

In 1948 Québec chose the fleur-de-lis as its national flag. Canon Groulx stated that this step constituted the most outstanding gesture marking the recognition of Québec as a French state. The symbolic event indeed marked the beginning of a period that would transform Québec society.

During the war and particularly after it, Québec experienced an exceptional rate of economic growth and social dislocation. In less than a single decade the province changed as much as it had during the whole of the previous century. The rate of industrial growth, for example, surpassed that of Canada as a whole; the labour force doubled; what was once a predominantly rural society became by the 1940s largely urban. According to two of Québec's leading economists, Faucher and Lamontagne, "there was a 92 per cent increase in the volume of goods manufactured in Québec, as compared to an 88 per cent increase for Canada as a whole; while industrial investment increased by 181 per cent in Québec, the comparable increase for Canada was only 154 per cent."[1] The economic and social changes were less noticeable at the time than the cultural and ideological shifts. The emerging social classes spawned by so major a transformation felt that Québec must catch up culturally and politically with the rest of Canada and the United States. They wanted the province to become an "Anglo-Saxon democracy." School attendance, for example, had become compulsory for all children. Professor Marcel Rioux described the era as one dominated by "l'idéologie de rattrapage" (the "let's-catch-up ideology").

In 1944 Maurice Duplessis once again came to power. He was suspicious, fearful and disdainful of intellectuals, whom he referred to as "piano players," and, not surprisingly, was unfavourable to the federal government's Massey Commission. He refused any official provincial co-operation with it when it was announced in 1949.

The Massey Report, nevertheless, stirred up considerable controversy within Québec's intelligentsia and gave rise to a debate on culture which persists to the present. The Massey-Lévesque Report, as it came to be known in Québec, divided the province's intellectuals into two main camps. The first group maintained that the soundest way to protect the cultural development of Québec was to let the *federal* government defend Canadian culture from the influences pouring in from the United States. The second group felt that *Québec* must develop its own cultural institutions, parallel to those being established by Ottawa, and that the province should exercise exclusive jurisdiction in this field to avoid becoming a mere tributary of the central source.

An editorial in a July 1951 edition of *Relations* summarized the conflicting points of view. The Jesuit journal expressed both satisfaction and concern with the situation: satisfaction with the Report because of its high intellectual and moral value and its sympathetic attitude toward the French fact. ("This is an attitude not often encountered in official reports originating in Ottawa," the author remarked, particularly "its open Canadian nationalism.") *Relations* was concerned, however, about the official recognition given this "Canadian" culture. This seemed a double threat: " ... the danger of government control of culture; most of the recommendations having been designed to encourage increasing government intervention," and "the danger of cultural centralism," since "the government referred to throughout the report is the federal government."

Father Lévesque had always emphasized the bicultural character of Canada, speaking of it as a land where two national cultures lived in *freedom*; this was to him the distinctive feature of Canadian civilization: " ... if we are to have freedom of culture, we must work harder to cultivate freedom."[2] According to his thesis, Canada's two cultures originated from civilizations where liberty had always flourished, from a common humanism. This view was not inconsistent with the education normally available in those days to the Québec elite, which concentrated on the humanities in "classical colleges." In 1954 Father Lévesque further defined his interpretation of the culture of French Canada: "It includes not only the province of Québec, but every area in which French culture lives, where the institutions that support it thrive, and where the language that expresses it is spoken." Lévesque went on to say that "since the French culture was a fact in Canada," the responsibility for its expression belonged to Canada as a whole.[3]

The two distinct streams of thought – the one relying on federalism to assist Québec cultural development, the other rejecting it in favour of a separate French effort – persisted, and a variety of opinions favouring an independent, politically and culturally autonomous Québec developed and attracted followers, while the moderates spoke to one another and to English Canada. As early as 1957, the more extreme and vocal supporters of the separatist viewpoint found a new home: L'Alliance laurentienne, a separatist political party, was created by Raymond Barbeau. It was the first of a series of Québec secessionist parties that was eventually to lead to René Lévesque's Sovereignty-Association movement in 1967, which in turn became the Parti Québécois in 1968 when it united the Rassemblement pour l'indépendance nationale (RIN) and the Ralliement national.

Several cultural groups tried to come to grips with the pace and direction of this cultural-political issue, and conferences were held in Québec during the fifties and early sixties when the province's intellectuals were increasingly taking positions on "the future of our nation." One debate was outstanding because of the representative nature and high quality of the speakers and their prominence in the community. L'Institut canadien des affaires publiques organized a conference in Ste-Adèle on September 22, 1955, on the topic: "Can the two cultures exist concurrently in Canada?" Father Lévesque took the affirmative, opposed by Professor Guy Frégault. The Québec newspaper of the intellectual and other influential elites of the province, *Le Devoir*, published the complete text of their speeches.[4]

In Father Lévesque's view, culture was primarily a "living, receptive thing," nourished from universal sources, and an integral part of man's life. Although having two cultures was a problem, it was also a valuable asset: "Riches are always a problem, but that is no reason to deprive oneself of them." As two cultures could not co-exist in the same country without influencing one another, they should take advantage of the situation and use it as a means of mutual enrichment. There was one essential condition: in each citizen, one culture "must come first and prevail over the other." This is what Fa-

82

ther Lévesque called "natural priority." The culture which prevailed in each individual would be "the one which was his own." For the English Canadian, the English culture would be dominant, and for the French Canadian, the French culture. When an individual lived away from his own cultural milieu, he had to superimpose his culture on the other "within himself."

Father Lévesque argued that the French-Canadian culture could remain vigorous despite its being surrounded by the influences of English culture. It could do so if it remained "master in its own house" and dominated outside influences: " ... to dominate is to select and assimilate." But first, one's culture had to be strong, strong enough to exercise this sort of influence over the forces of the other culture surrounding it. This, according to Lévesque, was where French-Canadian vitality and energy must be directed. He concluded on an optimistic note: "A strong and vital culture need not be afraid. Neither fanaticism, nor politics, nor money, nor even arms will prevail against it. The only enemy which can vanquish a culture is its own weakness."

The word nationalism, as it was used in Québec, could not easily be explained to English-speaking Canadians. In Father Lévesque's view, nationalism referred to Canada first, to the concept of one country, Canada, within which French culture would grow and develop, protected by the country as a whole. To others, such as Guy Frégault, nationalism was primarily a matter of culture and of language, a nation-wide *French*-Canadian nationalism which, if it did not strengthen its structures, would be threatened by Canadian nationalism. For Frégault the two nationalisms were seen as conflicting forces. To a small but growing group of extremists, nationalism meant Québec nationalism first and foremost; they felt the only way of preserving it was to separate it from Canadian nationalism which would always dominate it.

The difficulty over the word nationalism derives in part from its different interpretation by English- and French-speaking Canadians, especially in the fifties and sixties. When a Québécois speaks of Canada as two nations he is not thinking of two countries but of a distinct or unique country encompassing two principal ethnic groups, two languages, two cultures. When a Québécois hears an English-speaking Canadian speak of one nation he believes that the reference is to one single country inhabited by Canadians without any ethnic divisions of consequence – in other words, one country with two founding peoples. When Guy Frégault answered Father Lévesque, he began by observing that to be able to develop, a "national culture must be nourished and supported by a humane community that has at its disposal the resources, the institutions and especially the intellectual equipment needed to organize its territory, its politics, its economy, and its society."

In this perspective, it seemed obvious to him that French and English Canadians did not possess the same resources. He examined the cases of countries which had begun as European colonies. They had had to gain political autonomy before developing their own cultural identity. This was how Americans had managed to develop a distinct "intellectual personality," while English Canadians had tried to maintain their links with Great Britain. As for French Canada, although its ties with France were broken very early, Paris still dominated its culture to a great extent; the French-Canadian intellectual elite had little contact with the common man, and the gap between them was widening. Thus, both English and French Canadians had problems connected with their colonial status. Combining the two sets of problems did not seem a solution for either group. Nor had there been any evidence of spontaneous rapprochement between the two cultures. English Canada had never wanted the two cultures to overlap or integrate; it had, on the contrary, "always been sure to keep Québec in its place, which is that of a cultural enclave within a British nation."

The two leaders in the developing theory of French-Canadian cultural policy presented two totally different visions of the possibility of cultural development in Canada, ignoring entirely the increasing proportion of Canadians who thought of themselves and their cultures as being rooted elsewhere than in France or in Britain. The French-Canadian points of view were to dominate discussion of the issue for years. Frégault later referred to the confrontation in Ste-Adèle as "rather bitter." When Gérard Pelletier, the future federal Secretary of State, had asked Frégault to define himself, he had replied, "I am a French-Canadian nationalist."

During the fifties most Québec intellectuals argued for cultural independence in one form or another. Where they differed was in the means they thought should be used to assure it, one group assuming it could be done within the policies and institutions existing in Ottawa, the other certain that only homegrown and separately financed cultural organizations could serve Québec's needs. Thus, in 1957, with the establishment of the Canada Council, public opinion in Québec was again divided into two camps: one rejoicing in the opportunities the new federal institution would offer, the other opposing what they saw as dangerous or unconstitutional (or both) interference in Québec's cultural affairs. These divisions, this debate, persisted until the death of Maurice Duplessis gave them a new impetus. During his long regime no significant provincial institutions had been created to safeguard Québec's culture.

According to Canon Groulx in his memoirs, the province, at the time of Duplessis' death, experienced an underground earthquake: "Suddenly, it seemed, there was an explosion of aspirations too long repressed." Duplessis' successor as premier, Paul Sauvé, delivered his famous "from now on" speech, which had an electrifying effect within the province. A new era was being ushered in. But three months later Paul Sauvé, too, was dead: an event seen by many as a catastrophe.

But the impulse for change could not be arrested. The new generation could already be heard chanting the 1960 provincial election campaign slogan, "Maîtres chez nous," which was also to be used by the Liberal René Lévesque as a rallying cry for the nationalization of electric power companies in 1962-63. In the provincial election of 1960 following Sauvé's death, nearly fifteen years of conservative power came to an end. Jean Lesage became the first Liberal premier of Québec in a generation. It was the beginning of what came to be known as the Quiet Revolution. A new cultural policy had been a leading plank in Lesage's campaign. The study of the humanities was no longer the exclusive privilege of the elite; government loans and scholarships, in which federal assistance would play an important financial role, would soon open university doors to students from all social classes. A new Department of Education had as its slogan: "Qui s'instruit, s'enrichit." Hospital and health insurance funded in co-operation with the federal government would soon lighten the burden of sickness for the whole population. A new mood of optimism and euphoria swept Québec, where only a short while before Duplessis' well-known admonition to one of his colleagues had resounded: "Toé, tais-toé" (keep your mouth shut, you!)[5]

The years under Duplessis may not have been the age of darkness some have called them, yet cultural development in Québec under his administrations had been confined to small, protected (by Church or wealth or the French network of the CBC) intellectual elites, the small coteries of disciples of Henri Bourassa and of Canon

86

Lionel Groulx.[6] But from 1960 on, the lid was off and the movement of ideas and the debate of ideologies spread to a broader section of the population eager to participate. Guy Frégault, shortly before his premature death in 1977, gave this lyrical definition of the Quiet Revolution: "Now that it has been over for a long time, the Quiet Revolution must be seen for what it was: an exceptional development, as fragile and indestructible as hope, seemingly the result of an improbable set of circumstances, it was in fact the light at the end of a long, dark tunnel – a faint light, but one which glowed with the enduring promise of hope."[7] Frégault, himself one of the chief architects of the Quiet Revolution, has documented some of its significant aspects in an autobiographical account which bears the bittersweet title *Chronique des années perdues*. His book gives a moving account of the period from 1961 to 1966, when some of the most important provincial cultural institutions were created in Québec. Frégault was one of those whom Jean-Charles Falardeau had in mind when he wrote:

> ... the type of men who had been all but absent from our political history; men who through a bizarre linguistic mimesis, came to be known as the "great clerks" of State [of the Québec government]. There *had* been a certain number of them previously, several of whom were remarkable. But the difference was that this time, there were many more of them, and, more important, their competence was such that they immediately became the most important actors on the government scene (most of them, as we know, came from the academic world).[8]

It is often difficult, when dealing with history, to attempt to pinpoint beginnings precisely. But in the

Québec election of 1960 the first plank in the Liberal party platform referred to cultural development. Government cultural structures did begin to emerge in Québec in the spring of 1961, when the Department of Cultural Affairs was established under the guidance and direction of Georges-Emile Lapalme. Lapalme offered the position of deputy minister of cultural affairs to Guy Frégault, then a professor of history at the University of Ottawa. Frégault accepted. On March 2, 1961, Premier Jean Lesage stood up in the Québec Legislative Assembly and introduced the legislation establishing the Department of Cultural Affairs. "By establishing a Department of Cultural Affairs," he said, "the government of the province will be playing its proper role in the cultural life of Québec *and the nation.*"

In this way, the Québec of the Quiet Revolution expressed its wish for cultural self-determination but in the spirit of Bourassa and the Massey-Lévesque Report. Before 1961 Québec cultural institutions can hardly be described as having flourished as a result of previous provincial policies and aid. It would not be unfair to suggest that their sum total at the time of Lesage's announcement consisted of the St-Sulpice library, which did not yet have the courage to describe itself as the Québec National Library; the Québec Archives, later called the Archives nationales du Québec; the Conservatory of Music, which had not yet had the good fortune of being directed by Raoul Jobin; the dramatic arts section, which was struggling to survive under the leadership of that exceptional person Jean Valcourt; and the provincial museum, which was beginning to be known as the Musée du Québec under the able direction of Gérard Morisset.

These institutions, which were to become the embryo of the new Department of Cultural Affairs, obviously suffered from penury, lack of status and authority. In 1960, the province which historically had shown the deepest concern for its cultural future for centuries before Confederation was, as in so many other aspects of its life, an underdeveloped area within Canada. But this did not prevent Premier Lesage and his team from thinking about the "French fact in America." André Laurendeau, one of Duplessis' "piano players," commented: "If Québec becomes the national government of French Canadians, as Ottawa is essentially the national government of Canadians, it will do so without having the same authority or the same financial resources to draw upon." He went on: "If matters did not change in Ottawa, if on the contrary the situation in Québec developed as planned, then things would become intolerable. The realization would gradually dawn on us that our 'national state' was incomplete, relatively poor and constantly limited in its initiatives."[9]

And so, in starting to provide itself with a cultural framework and governmental infrastructure, Québec advanced toward discovering itself as "the political expression of French Canada." It was not long before the province opened its arms to francophone minorities like the Acadians, whose sad and proud history the Québécois had always found especially moving. As Guy Frégault expressed it, we tend "to see the Acadians as Québécois who have had a particularly rough time of it." Québec delegates were sent to New Brunswick and to Nova Scotia to attend conferences and inaugurations; and in 1965, the Québec government came to the financial support of the Acadian newspaper *L'Evangéline* with a $100,000 grant.

Residents of the Maritimes were not the only ones to feel Québec's presence; so did the province's other neighbours, the Franco-Ontarians, who, according to Frégault, were "less complicated than the Acadians: they are transplanted Québécois." Québec's presence was felt particularly in the Franco-Ontarian communities' cultural events and representative organizations. Frégault's message to them, at least in his first years at the new department, was that a French Canada was only viable if Québec were strong and healthy. In addition he wished Québec to establish closer links with intellectuals in Ontario sensitive to the aspirations of French-Canadian culture. Frégault observed that "Toronto is much more open to the manifestations of Québécois culture than is British Montréal."[10] He understood, too well perhaps, where the elitists' noses were pointed in the fresh easterly winds.

Breaking out of the ghetto fostered during the Duplessis years and seeking ties with colleagues in other parts of Canada was only one manifestation of the new outward-looking optimism stimulated by the Quiet Revolution. Québec also began to open up to the world at large. In 1961, the Québec "Délégation générale" was opened in Paris, with André Malraux in attendance. Under the direction of Charles Lussier, the Québec delegation was active organizing exhibitions, symposia, conferences, music festivals and cultural exchanges. During the same year a similar "office" was opened in New York. Relations between Québec and Louisiana became increasingly strong and cordial. The following year a Québec delegation was installed in London. And Québec began to send cultural emissaries abroad. In the spring of 1962, the Montréal Symphony Orchestra prepared for an extensive European tour assisted by the Canada Council; there was an exhibition of the works of Québécois painters in Spoleto, and Québec art critics took part in a major international conference in Amsterdam. On September 1, 1963, the Service du Canada français d'outre-frontières (French Canada Service Abroad) was established, and under its auspices relations between Québec and Africa were initiated. Throughout this period, and in the face of these major cultural activities of the province, the federal government showed greater concern about the outward trappings of these activities and the embarrassing conclusions that might be drawn from them by the outside world than in developing its own cultural policies to accommodate and connect with this exciting expression of a previously restrained and largely provincially impoverished cultural group.

"The feds" need not have worried: the financial means at the disposal of the Department of Cultural Affairs were not commensurate with its aspirations. It had an initial budget of less than $3 million. In 1963 this was increased to $5 million and by 1968, in spite of increasing rates of inflation, the figure was just over $12 million. The slow growth of staff was an added impediment which delayed the establishment and operation of services.

Nevertheless, even in the early sixties there was progress. The Provincial Arts Council was set up in 1961, with the distinguished Laval Professor Jean-Charles Falardeau as its first president. Later, he was to look back at the early days and remember them as a period when the Council "breakfasted on morning sunlight but had to sup on shooting stars."[11] But it rarely, if ever, met.

April 1962 saw the birth of the Office de la langue française, under the direction of Jean-Marc Léger. In theory, few would deny that language is central to culture; in Québec, as in France, in practice, language and culture are indissoluble. The aim of the Office, in 1963 was "to encourage the use of international French"; by 1964, it was to "ensure the normal development of French." At this time the concept of "Canadianismes de bon aloi" (linguistically sound Canadianisms) was born, and in 1963 – 64, the "norme du français écrit et parlé au Québec" (Quebec standard of written and spoken French) was established. This led to a slogan which ex-

91

pressed the Province's new linguistic and cultural self-assertion: "Ici on parle français."

Publishing was another area crying out for help. The Québec book situation in the fifties and sixties was an alarming one. On January 24, 1964, Mr. Lapalme introduced in the Québec Legislative Assembly a report prepared by a commission of inquiry into the Québec book trade, the Bouchard Report. The Conseil supérieur du livre was set up and continuing consultation established with the department which provided a secretariat to assist the co-ordination of several professional groups such as the Société des editeurs canadiens, the Société des editeurs de manuels scolaires and the Société des librairies. The statistics seemed appalling: 80 per cent of bookstore stocks in Québec were imported and the prices of the imported product were beyond the reach of most pockets. The Bouchard Report had tried to deal with the inevitable difficulties in publishing in the relatively small market of Québec and had recommended ways to make books more accessible to the Québec public, particularly those in the French language and by French-Canadian authors. But apart from the few institutional and bureaucratic changes started by Lapalme, the chief outcome took the form of more studies and reports with little improvement in the situation apart from minor subsidization of student textbooks.

By 1964 a policy came to the fore of making Québec culture more accessible – democratization, as future federal Secretaries of State would call it. In theatre, the policy resulted in two impressive capital achievements. In mid-July 1964, an act was passed with respect to the Place des Arts: Québec and Montréal jointly assumed financial responsibility for the centre, and together appointed the members of its administrative board. Next came the Grand Théâtre de Québec, established in response to an obvious need in the provincial capital. After much deliberation and tribulation it was completed in 1968.

Museums were also seen as essential to the dissemination of culture. A new wing was added to the Musée du Québec in 1964 and the influence of this museum was felt increasingly in other institutions in the Québec City area. (The Musée du Québec has continued to grow, and a proposal of the Lévesque administration to transform it further into the National Museum of Québec has received serious consideration.) A museum of modern art (Musée d'art contemporain) was established in Montréal for the purpose of acquiring and developing a collection of works created after 1940. Although the foundation of this project was laid on June 1, 1964, the official inauguration of the Museum, at the Château Dufresne, only came a year later. Guy Robert was the gallery's first director and under his aggressive guidance it developed rapidly. It began with a modest budget of $100,000, looking to private support to expand its collection. It was later moved from Montréal's east end, a location chosen in accordance with the government's cultural decentralization policy, to the Cité du Havre, some distance from the centre of the city and in consequence lost an important portion of the public it had been carefully nurturing.

But Montréal's foremost cultural institution remained the Museum of Fine Arts on Sherbrooke Street in the heart of Montréal's English-speaking business district. Guy Frégault spoke bitterly of the Museum in the following terms: "It is a very beautiful creation of the English-speaking aristocracy. It has been noted, and accurately so, that the latter group is the one which shows the keenest sensitivity, the greatest persistence and the most intelligent enthusiasm in its efforts to preserve Québec's past and present cultural heritage." The Québécois had never felt at home there; it seemed they experienced a certain chill, as they might "among the marble columns and counters of a bank."[12]

By the mid-sixties the Department of Cultural Affairs had generated intense activity, and some of its accomplishments were seen to be impressive. Curiously enough, while the main provisions of the Act of 1961 had been implemented by then, it was at this time that the man behind most of these accomplishments chose to resign. Georges-Emile Lapalme wrote to Jean Lesage on September 3, 1964, announcing his intention to leave. It was no secret that his departure was prompted by his frustration with the government's persistent refusal to provide his department with anything like reasonable financial support. He was succeeded by Pierre Laporte, who was determined not to be driven from office for the same reason. In September 1965 Laporte announced a reorganization of the Department of Cultural Affairs. Among various changes in its structure and responsibilities was the addition of the Immigration Branch. Laporte explained the new appendage in the following terms: "It is high time that the government began to concern itself with receiving immigrants and integrating them into the French-speaking milieu, instead of standing by helplessly, observing their tendency to join, almost to a man, the dominant minority."[13]

Once again Québec revealed its perception of the importance of culture to its political policies and to the development of a sense of community. The new minister felt that by organizing and controlling the immigration service, his department would be holding an additional important lever of Québec's cultural policy.

In Québec, then, where the anxieties loosed by modernization were most acute, the centrality of culture was understood very well by its political and intellectual leaders. The whole of Québec's history since the Conquest had been concerned with the defence of its language, religion and culture. Modernization brought, as it did everywhere, a new self-awareness and consciousness of the threat to identity. Federal grants to universities had posed an acute constitutional problem. Pierre Elliott Trudeau and Gérard Pelletier had been prominent among those who believed that while Duplessis had starved the universities, it was new, democratic, outward-looking provincial governments that were needed rather than federal intervention in provincial jurisdiction.[14]

As in many European countries, accelerating modernization was experienced as Americanization. The entire population of Canada, or nearly all of it, lives within three hundred miles of the United States border and is wide open to the powerful engine of American mass communications and the American-based multinational corporations. More than the populations of any European country, the Canadian population tended to become Americanized (though the French-Canadian population felt they were being Anglicized). During the 1960s the intellectual elites of Québec and of English-speaking Canada increasingly felt the threat to a distinctive Canadian identity – and perhaps to their own ideas of leadership in Toronto and Montréal. In Ontario it was the patrician conservative scholar, George Grant, who was moved to publish his often bitter *Lament for a Nation*, in which he suggested that continentalism – as the surrender to Americanizing modernization began to be called – was based on the liberal view of history which identifies democracy with the American kind, "equality, contractual human relations, and the society open to all men, regardless of race or creed or class." In Grant's threnody the Canadian nation was already dead, sacrificed for the profits of a Liberal alliance with continental business.[15] But, as one reviewer recognized, "If there is a great deal of ruin in all nations [due to the homogenizing effect of United States' influence], Canada has more to spare

95

than most." And Professor Grant seemed to have noticed this and taken it into account when he published his book of exciting and provocative essays, *Technology and Empire*, four years later. While he continues his theme that Canadian independence is hardly possible, swept as our country inevitably must be into the American vortex, the passion with which he describes the loss of values in this U.S.-dominated world, "where technological progress becomes itself the sole context within which all that is other to it must attempt to be present," is softened. "Nothing here written implies that the increasingly difficult job of preserving what is left of Canadian sovereignty is not worth the efforts of practical men."[15]

But Grant's thesis relates most deeply to his belief that we are witnesses to the end of Western Christianity and whatever the merits of his argument, it seemed to herald the growth of a new consciousness of the vital role of culture in national life, and of increasing demands from artists and intellectuals that Canadian governments should do something more about it. It did not matter that great wealth married to the most advanced technology required no conscious motivation to cross borders or oceans. It is notable that in those European countries which were feeling the same threat to identity from Americanization, governments began to take an increasingly energetic role in supporting national culture: in Germany at the municipal level, in France through the comprehensive policy of André Malraux, de Gaulle's minister of culture, in Britain through publicly financed but independent bodies like the Arts Council.

Another way of looking at the threat of Americanization is to see that the competition of the free market tends to result in conformity and homogeneity; products tend to become like their competing products; and this homogeneity of the material culture is soon reflected in spiritual conformity. The role of governments is increasingly to correct this tendency by support to minority interests and preferences, to protect eccentric individuals and communities from the tyranny of the majority.

The years that followed the Massey-Lévesque Report were of enormous prosperity and expansive confidence.[16] It was assumed in the late 1950s and early 1960s that education was the royal road to the future, that every university graduate would add dollars to the gross national product, that advanced studies would be the occupation of many citizens. The number of Canadian universities multiplied with funds from federal and provincial sources; student enrollment increased by tens of thousands as the generation of the postwar baby boom grew up. Adult education classes flourished; it was the era of continuing education. All Canadians, apparently, could participate in the Canadian dream. But who was "all"?

In Québec especially, there were other dimensions to modernization. The Quiet Revolution, as we have noted, was a cultural upheaval at once universal and domestic. The Catholic Church was going through its crisis of renewal; small matters seemed of great moment (the clergy giving up their traditional cassocks for common clothes, for example) and the great matters discussed at Vatican II were both frightening and liberating. New ideas and myths and leaders emerged from the mass media. From 1950 on, several French-Canadian poets proselytized the recognition of the "land" as their predecessors had done in the nineteenth century and came to be known as "the Hexagone" group. And while many writers and artists still tended to leave the province, like Pierrette Alarie, Léopold Simoneau, Kenneth Gilbert, Claire Martin to mention a few, there were still others who stayed home and threw themselves into the excitement of politics.

The connection between culture and political survival had always been clear in the French-speaking province. It was perceived by governments and people alike and the connection was becoming clearer to some. But Québec was not the whole of Canada and the new directions which the Quiet Revolution had only begun to reflect there, seemed to have less rather than more in common with stirrings in other parts of the country. Technology and affluence would further acerbate and exasperate what appeared on the surface as an improving situation.

As in an earlier period when the railway and telegraph, instead of drawing Canada together, had tended to decentralize it, so now the new media of radio and television, once firmly established with wide coverage, made Québec more self-consciously French and all other regions correspondingly more self-absorbed; at the same time the new electronic technology and opportunities for private profit in Canada increased the opportunity and pace of Americanization. The CBC launched Canadian television late in 1952, with separate programming in French and English. While broadcasting in both languages was inevitable and necessary, the resulting creation of two solitudes in production was not.

Perhaps in response to the influence of advertising, whose visible metaphors on television were increasingly sensual, the old, cold-water-drinking Puritan Canadians were being turned into pleasure lovers. Puritanism would return under the banners of conservationism or feminism or hypochondria later, but it would never be the same again. Licensing laws were relaxed during the 1960s and soon the larger cities would cater to the most discriminating epicures. And these boom years made it possible for affluent Canadians to spend their money in new ways. Sexual taboos weakened to the point where, in some cities, a good many older people were frightened. A whole generation freaked out on drugs and hard rock, and these interior "trips" were matched by the travels all over the world of vacationing Canadians. Small-l liberalism had become so widely accepted that liberals themselves became uneasy and began to search for positions that made them feel more like the tigers they had thought themselves in the late 1950s.

It was the period of McLuhan, that Canadian oracle of the new age of television and education, a steadfast Catholic traditionalist many of whose rhapsodies of trivia and trivial rhapsodies were widely misunderstood – except by the advertising industry.[17]

We have seen how long and how cautiously the federal government took to back into founding the Canada Council, even though Prime Minister St. Laurent, shortly after the launching of Canadian television in 1952, had told Gérard Pelletier, then a reporter: "I had thought that it would be a stone around my neck; I found out during this election [1953] that it was a halo over my head!"[18]

No doubt the habit of establishing art institutions as independent Crown corporations owed at least as much to the politicians' fear of having to answer for the high-jinks of artists as it did to the need to keep the arts free from political interference. In Canada, too, there was apparent conflict between the need for social justice and the need for cultural development. We may be reminded of the example of Judas, who objected to the expense when his Master was given a vial of precious ointment; he felt the money should have been given to the poor.

Fears that the electorate might be hostile to cultural spending by the federal government in these years were probably unfounded. On the contrary, there is evidence that a silent majority had come to welcome cultural projects. Lesage's cultural moves had been applauded. Mayor Drapeau of Montréal, who was probably the first municipal leader to provide a regular fund for a

Canadian city's budget to support community arts activities, repeatedly involved his city in grandiose cultural ventures and was attacked by almost everyone in Canada who had a voice, for putting circuses before bread. Each time he was vindicated at the polls. Whether we like this example or not, the lesson is clear. The electorate endorsed ventures that made them feel proud of their community.

Early in 1963 the newly elected federal Liberal government under Lester Pearson decided to make a new and vigorous approach to the problem of support for the arts and other cultural activities. The man behind this approach, interestingly enough, was an intellectual francophone economist, Maurice Lamontagne, who had just been elected to Parliament for the first time and who had been a leading architect of the Liberal campaign that, so he and the party brass claimed, was going to change Canada – and its culture – in sixty days. The portfolio chosen for this new responsibility was that of the Secretary of State, one of the few that had existed continuously since Confederation, when it was intended to be a sort of department of federal-provincial affairs. Nothing much had come of this. The department comprised (until 1966) the Registrar General of Canada, the Translation Bureau, a small protocol section, the Companies Branch and the Patent Office.

In April 1963 the portfolio was transformed by the transfer to it of a number of cultural agencies, followed by others in succeeding months. These were the Canada Council, the National Gallery, the National Museums, the National Library and Public Archives, the Board of Broadcast Governors and the Canadian Broadcasting Corporation, the National Film Board, the Queen's Printer, and the Centennial Commission (which included the nucleus of the staff transferred to the National Arts Centre in 1968). The Citizenship and Citizenship Regis-

100

tration branches were added in the general reorganization of 1966.

The problems to be faced were complex and various. In general, the funds available for cultural activities were inadequate and some of the statutes governing the cultural institutions were long out of date. Under J. W. Pickersgill, Maurice Lamontagne, and Judy LaMarsh, successive Secretaries of State from 1963 to 1968, three main lines of action were developed to provide a firmer base for the future enunciation of a comprehensive federal cultural policy.

First, pressure was exerted to obtain more money, with increasingly successful results: the most notable being for the Canada Council. Until 1965 the Canada Council could budget no more than $1.5 million a year for support for the arts (the balance going to the humanities and social sciences), this being the arts' share of the Council's income from its original endowment. In March 1965, a grant of $10 million was made which was intended to be spent over three fiscal years (thus, incidentally, overwhelming its initial modest budget) but, with Cabinet approval, was spent in two. It had become obvious that even the additional funds were inadequate to meet demands from the arts community. Thus, in 1966 the Secretary of State, Maurice Lamontagne, prodded and assisted by Jean Boucher, the Director of the Canada Council, sought and received from Parliament extra funds – beginning with $16.9 million in 1967-68 – henceforth on an annual vote. It was clear that this annual subsidy would make the Council more directly dependent on the government and expose it to political criticism. Some feared it might expose it also to political direction; this did not occur, even in the sensitive areas of the social sciences and humanities. The Canada Council from the outset had responded to initiatives from voluntary agencies and in doing so it developed, naturally enough, a constituency. The transition from patronage by elites, governors general and private corporations to public patronage directed by professional culture-bureaucrats was gradual and is perhaps not yet complete.

Secondly, a start was made on new legislation for the National Gallery and its incorporation into a new National Museums institution, which was now to include a Museum of Science and Technology; in the event, all were covered by the National Museums Act proclaimed in 1968 to rationalize the administration of institutions which were to have enhanced resources to respond to the new consciousness of our heritage partly attributed to the success of Expo '67. A new National Library Act was similarly developed, taking into account that books were no longer the only possible contents of a library. The Secretary of State was heavily involved, also, with the development of the National Arts Centre, the national Centennial project. The team working on this was at first attached to the Centennial Commission but the ensuing antipathies led to its transfer to the department in 1965. The Centre, built at a cost of some $44 million, rather larger than Parliament and the public had anticipated, was transferred to a Board of Trustees by the National Arts Centre Act proclaimed in 1966.

Thirdly, the federal institutions relating to larger audiences were also not ignored. The state of the Canadian film industry called for urgent attention, as did the running feud between the NFB and the CBC on the subject of feature film production. A committee chaired by Dr. O. J. Firestone was set up to examine the problems and make recommendations. The outcome was the enactment in 1967 of the Canadian Film Development Corporation Bill establishing a body to promote the production of feature films in Canada. Preparations were also begun for a new National Film Act, but these lapsed while a

102

series of new inquiries was set in motion from 1968 on.

Broadcasting, however, presented the most complex and intractable problem of all. The CBC had been harassed for years by a series of public inquiries, culminating in strong criticism by the 1961 Special Parliamentary Committee on Broadcasting and, in 1962, by the Glassco Commission. The Board of Broadcast Governors (BBG) was thought by many to have failed in its control of private television, and there were many who believed that the CBC should abandon all advertising. On this question, the so-called Troika Committee (Dr. Andrew Stewart of the BBG, Alphonse Ouimet of the CBC and Don Jamieson of the Canadian Association of Broadcasters) submitted three separate reports early in 1964, each in disagreement with both of the others. In May 1964, shortly following his entry into the Cabinet as Secretary of State, Maurice Lamontagne appointed an Advisory Committee on Broadcasting, chaired by Robert Fowler, a tycoons' bureaucrat from Montréal who had been chairman of the 1955 Royal Commission. (This was to lead to confusion between what were known as the Fowler Commission and the Fowler Committee.) For reasons that have never been adequately explained, the terms of reference explicitly excluded cablevision, already seen as a potential threat to conventional broadcasting.

After consideration of the report submitted by the Fowler Committee in the fall of 1965, a White Paper on Broadcasting was issued in June 1966, followed by the new Broadcasting Act proclaimed in 1968. While the government accepted the underlying philosophy of the Committee's report, few of its recommendations were actually implemented. The new act contained what had been lacking in its 1958 predecessor, a declaration of national broadcasting policy which included explicit objectives for the CBC. The BBG was replaced by the much larger Canadian Radio-Television Commission, with similar powers. The change of name was, in a sense, little more than cosmetic, but facilitated a much more active approach to regulation under the chairmanship of Pierre Juneau and the beginning of an activism on the part of this semi-judicial regulatory authority into the relatively vacant field of policy making.[19]

Another new policy development of the early 1960s was based on the notion that it would be helpful to have some sort of organized "loyal opposition" to act as a sounding-board for new programs and policies, and to provide the minister with points of contact in bodies representing all or some of the arts. The first grants were made to such groups as the Canadian Broadcasting League, the Canadian Museums Association and the Canadian Conference of the Arts. In 1964 Maurice Lamontagne was credited with being the first federal minister ever to sit down and talk to a representative body of artists when he attended the annual meeting of the Canadian Conference of the Arts at Ste-Adèle, Québec. The meeting turned out to be a turning point in the development of federal cultural policy, for an angry outcry against the lassitude of the Centennial Commission with regard to its arts program resulted in a much larger provision for the performing arts (although no more than token provision was ever forthcoming for the visual arts program).

The outcome of this new approach to cultural activities was not, as the press feared, the establishment of a cultural commissar. While at first the Secretary of State, loaded down with this grab-bag of cultural institutions, may have appeared to resemble Stephen Leacock's man who jumped on his horse and rode off in all directions, the outcome was not chaos but the beginning of a much needed though limited degree of rationalization. The minister speaks in Parliament for these agencies and

104

must approve their estimates, but he is not authorized to meddle in their internal affairs. His department is therefore something much less than a ministry of culture and information. The typical cultural agency is a Crown corporation under the authority of an appointed board of citizens chosen from various regions and walks of life.

But this rapid change of pace and availability of new funds had an impact on Parliament and the decision-making process of the federal Cabinet. In June 1965, recognizing the increasing importance of federally financed cultural activities, particularly broadcasting, Pearson agreed to the establishment by Parliament of a Standing Committee on Broadcasting, Film, and Assistance to the Arts. It did not sit until the following February when, under the chairmanship of Gérard Pelletier (Ron Basford was vice-chairman and members included Gordon Fairweather and David Lewis), it was entirely occupied with first the Fowler Report and then the "Seven Days" crisis at the CBC.

Of greater significance as a symbol of the increase in federal attention demanded by cultural affairs was the establishment by the new Prime Minister, Pierre Trudeau, in the spring of 1969 of a Cabinet Committee on Culture and Information. In Pearson's time, no such formal decision-making mechanism existed within the cabinet system. When Secretary of State Lamontagne decided he needed money for the Centennial, the construction of the National Arts Centre or the re-financing of the Canada Council, he simply cleared it with the Prime Minister, ensured himself of the support of the Minister of Finance of the day or the President of the Treasury Board, and took the issue directly to Cabinet for rubber stamping. There had been ad hoc committees on broadcasting and even one on the issue of educational television, but no permanent mechanisms of consultation were built upon these experiences. Until Miss LaMarsh began to experience difficulty with several of her Cabinet colleagues shortly before she ceased to be Secretary of State, she too tended to have the policies and financing of her department dealt with in much the same manner as her predecessor.

The new structures for Cabinet decision-making introduced by Trudeau changed all this. A Cabinet Committee on Culture and Information, chaired by the Secretary of State, was given an Assistant Secretary to the Cabinet responsible to the Cabinet's Deputy Secretary (Operations) as its Secretary. The first incumbent was Paul Tellier whose task it was not only to assist the ministers of the Committee and provide them and the chairman with advice on all matters pertaining to the various missions of the Department of the Secretary of State, but also on other major cultural areas like communications, government information policies and official languages. Within a year of its first meeting in October 1969, the whole subject area of "science" had been added to the Committee's responsibilities and the new Department of Communications had become firmly established. There was thus less and less time for the detailed examination of the expanding programs in the Department of the Secretary of State. There is even less time now, since the Committee's work has been subsumed under another new Cabinet committee dealing with Cultural and Native Affairs.

In 1963 the Royal Commission on Bilingualism and Biculturalism, under the joint chairmanship of Davidson Dunton and André Laurendeau, was appointed, originally on the nineteenth-century assumption of Canada as a pact between the founding races of British and French origin. This assumption was quickly corrected by Pearson when it became obvious that, particularly in the prairies, Canadians of other ethnic origins were not willing to have their part in the building of modern Canada

106

overlooked. The fact of this oversight is symbolic of the insensitivity of Canadian governments to what Marius Barbeau once described in speaking of the francophone minority as "the vitality of ancestral traditions coupled with isolation." The Commission's public hearings, preliminary report, multi-volume report and final recommendations were to take up a large part of the government's energy and resources in the cultural area for years to come. Among the reluctant discoveries of this Commission was the fact of multiculturalism in Canada, a notion of Canadian culture which eventually came to be accepted as a reality by all federal political parties.

André Laurendeau had been one of the chief architects of Québec's developing self-consciousness in the late fifties and early sixties. As editor-in-chief of *Le Devoir*, leaving partisan politics behind him, he had won the respect of Québécois well beyond the circulation of his newspaper. Throughout his life he had been engaged in a passionate search for a formula that could ensure the equality of Québec's status with that of the rest of Canada. When, in July 1963, he agreed to become co-chairman of the B&B Commission, he was undertaking a task, the purpose of which he had been advocating since the beginning of 1962, and the satisfactory outcome of which he was then fairly certain was attainable. But some years after his premature death, *Le Devoir* published (June 1, 1978) for the first time selected extracts from the personal diary he kept while travelling for the Commission between 1964 and 1967. In some of his lines one senses the deep bitterness growing in his soul as he continued to confront the realities of ignorance and prejudice each day, and which provoked in him "a veritable inner push toward separatism" (de véritables poussées intérieures vers le séparatisme.) He writes, in some despair, about the isolation in which he is likely to find himself as a federalist in Québec, facing his friends and the young.

107

Nevertheless, he categorically reaffirmed his faith in federalism: "only one thing is more repugnant to me than being booed by the young and that is to flatter the young demagogically. Here is a new situation where I will be condemned to solitude. Life will never smile at me again."

The B&B, as the Commission came to be referred to by critics and supporters alike, was the most important federal investigation into a basic cultural subject since the Massey Commission. It dealt with French and English as "official" languages, with the status of these languages in the private and public work world, with the development and protection of these languages in the educational system (in spite of the jurisdictional problem) and with the problems of the place of language – and thus culture – in Parliament, the Cabinet and the Supreme Court. Where language was spoken, there was the Commission. It was everywhere and into everything: voluntary associations, ethnic groups and the world of the media, arts and letters. Though the quality of its numerous volumes was uneven, they did more than announce that "Canada, without being fully conscious of the fact, is passing through the greatest crisis in its history" which if left uncorrected would lead to the break-up of the country.

Like Massey before them, Dunton, Laurendeau and their colleagues revealed the basic connection between culture and politics and reminded Canadians that only by recognizing the centrality of this particular cultural issue to the political crisis could they preserve the national integrity of their country. However, while the Commission recognized the issue, the solutions it proposed focused on the narrower function of language. The general and central point was missed by Parliament, by legislatures, and by the majority of Canadians, and the significance of the issue never again seized the country as a whole until the election of an indépendantist government in Québec produced Bill 101.

One should not be too surprised, therefore, at this Ottawa response since federal parliamentarians have rarely shown much interest in the fundamental role of cultural activity. A similar response awaited another major investigation into a fundamental area of culture, the voluminous Report (and studies) of the Special Senate Committee on Science Policy, which was established in 1967 to examine the future of science policy in Canada[20] and the possibilities of appraising priorities, organization and budgets in this field.

Nevertheless, such investigations highlighted the need to develop a comprehensive policy in cultural matters and showed that the urge to rationalize was at last beginning to permeate the leadership cadres. Some vigorous action began, not only at the federal level but also in the provinces. But there were many people in the country, by no means all jocks or philistines, who were still asking why we should do all these things. Was it to improve the quality of life for Canadians? To strengthen the symbolic bonds of nationhood and of unity? To give Canadians experiences they could be proud of? The questions were legitimate, the answers by governments hardly forthcoming.

All this became clearer in the national euphoria excited by the international success of Expo 67 in Montréal, celebrating a hundred years of Confederation. The country had looked forward to it gloomily. It would never work; it would disgrace us all; it would never be open on time; the island on which it was sited would sink. But when it did open on time, astonishing the world by its quality, Canadians immediately forgot their fears and forebodings and, unfortunately, the men who had made it a success.

Expo 67 was a cultural festival, the climax of the

109

Centennial celebrations. Canadian architects, designers, engineers, artists, film makers, poets, actors, writers, craftsmen, publicists, saw themselves – and were seen by their countrymen – in an international showcase that revealed them as second to none.

It would be hard to overestimate the bright hopes and national self-confidence kindled by this collective effort of Canada's cultural community that was running in parallel with the forebodings of the B&B. Not since victory in the Second World War had Canadians held their heads so high, or looked at each other with so much mutual respect and sense of nationality. The budget of the Centennial Commission alone had represented, according to Robert Fulford,[21] the largest single infusion of hard cash in the history of Canadian culture (except for CBC allocations), to the visual and performing arts. The Department of National Defence spent nearly $7 million running two trains which criss-crossed the country presenting their famous tattoos. The whole of the Centennial project, and especially Expo 67, had proved that investment in culture could be more than justified by the national awareness and self-confidence it generated. Few noticed, however, that while the site was in Montréal, some francophone Québécois were far from sharing the euphoria of the rest of the country. October 1970 was a short three years away and the postal-box bombings were at hand.

The larger lesson of Expo and the fears of the B&B commissioners were to go unheeded by many in power not only in Ottawa but also in the West and in Québec, where the pace of economic and social change was reaching new heights. The special moment when the people seemed united in the enjoyment of the things they had built together and cherished was allowed to pass.

It is scarcely necessary to remark that a stationary condition of capital and population implies no stationary state of human improvement. There would be as much scope as ever for all kinds of mental culture and moral and social progress; as much room for improving the Art of Living, and much more likelihood of its being improved, when minds cease to be engrossed by the art of getting on.

John Stuart Mill, 1848.

The Civil Service of the country, though not the animating spirit, is the living mechanism through which the body politic moves and breathes and has its being. Upon it depends the rapid and economical conduct of every branch of your affairs; and there is nothing about which a nation should be so particular as to secure in such a service independence, zeal, patriotism and integrity.

Lord Dufferin, 1878.

We forget that the measure of the value of a nation to the world is neither the bushel nor the barrel, but mind; and that wheat and pork, though useful and necessary, are but dross in comparison with those intellectual products which alone are imperishable.

Sir William Osler, 1892.

Culture is what remains when all else is forgotten.

Selma Lagerlöf, 1909.

With the Greek, let us measure our contribution to civilization in what we give to the humanities.

W. L. Mackenzie King, 1914.

The economist can, of course, give us the facts. That is his job. He is a good cartographer, but a bad pilot. There were plenty of crises in the nineteenth century, when cold-blooded economic fact would have been the end of us if there had not been some vision to interpret it.

Vincent Massey, 1924.

There are only two kinds of government – the scarcely tolerable and the absolutely unbearable.

John W. Dafoe.

FIVE

I have suggested that in the first hundred years of Confederation Canadians conducted their common life by the light of certain mental habits; and that these were habits of mutual toleration, restraint and liberty. That they were also habits of staying in our own cultural backyards may be explained by the facts of geography, history and demography that preceded Confederation as well as by the provisions of a constitution which has given us a dozen educational systems and two official languages.

The discovery of our ethnic pluralism came late, but like the distinctive perception of Québec culture by Francophones, it had always existed. The approach of Canadian governments and, more accurately, of a few interested prime ministers, to cultural policy was hesitant, but invariably marked by a belief that the state should have no part in the direction of culture. There was never an official culture, and the characteristic form of federal public cultural institutions was the Crown corporation. The Public Archives, the National Gallery of Canada and the Canadian Broadcasting Corporation were early

113

examples of the type of organization Canadian governments believed best served federal patronage of cultural activity. In recommending the foundation of the Canada Council, the Massey Report had said, "We should also consider it a misfortune if the Canada Council became in any sense a department of government, but we realize that since this body will be spending public money it must be in an effective manner responsible to the Government and hence to Parliament." But each painfully slow step by government to assist the arts – perhaps in part as a result of this "arms-length" habit of administration – was taken in isolation and soon forgotten. The official mind hardly developed the consciousness necessary to take full advantage of the results of establishing great Canadian cultural organizations like the CBC or the Canada Council, or to foresee the long-term implications of large technical machines affecting the popular imagination. The special opportunity offered by rare expressions of our national character like Expo 67 remained unappreciated.

Nevertheless, by the centenary of Confederation the Department of the Secretary of State was beginning to discharge some of the functions of a ministry of culture and to move toward their rationalization. The minister, still regarded by his colleagues, Parliament and the media as "junior," was already accountable to Parliament and public for a substantial budget spent on several large federal cultural institutions whose work touched upon some of the most fundamental aspects of Canadian life. Behind this growing importance of the ministry was an explosion of information about Canada demanded by the public and paid for by the federal treasury. The reports of Massey, Fowler, Dunton-Laurendeau and Lamontagne have been mentioned; and there were others.

This chapter surveys the present state of government support to culture, which developed in the optimistic atmosphere of the late sixties and early seventies and in some degree in response to the reports just mentioned. I shall try to make sense of it.

Gérard Pelletier became Secretary of State in 1968. He was impressed by the need for a comprehensive cultural policy. No minister was better equipped than he by education, work experience, depth of knowledge of many cultures and of many styles of government. No Secretary of State was better placed to carry out his views; he was the Prime Minister's closest friend and his familiar sage. No Privy Councillor was so cultivated or so articulate in both official languages and hence in so favoured a position to explain his policies to all Canadians. The 1960s had been a period of agitation and demands for participation in public decision-making. Influenced not only by the example of France and the efforts of his friend the French Minister of Culture, André Malraux, but also by the new drive and ferment in Québec, Pelletier announced a policy of "democratization and decentralization." Though he encouraged the National Museums of Canada to apply the policy soon after he came to his post, it was clear that he meant it to have wider application. The Liberal election campaign of 1968 was riddled with such portentous phrases as the "just society" and "participatory democracy," and the philosophy of the new Secretary of State had its roots in his and his party leader's determination to apply these doctrines to the cultural scene.[1]

But it was a far more complex problem to apply these ideas to culture than appeared on the surface. Democratization and decentralization could not be achieved without either massive infusions of new dollars or transfers of long-standing financial commitments from established social programs since the government had already indicated publicly its concern about the high level of public expenditures and its desire to see these reduced.

115

But the geography of the country, the uneven development of cultural resources in the regions, the uniqueness and pace of socio-cultural developments first in Québec and then in the West, the enormous overflow of American cultural products into every part of the country and the weak base in Ottawa from which to decentralize, all made large expenditure inevitable. How a practicable and just distribution of resources was to be determined was never raised, though the success of such a policy depended (and depends) on an informed and sensitive answer to such a question. How each province was likely to respond and how their existing cultural institutions would be affected was never clear. How masses of people were to learn how to enjoy elements of high culture was never even a subject of discussion – at any level. That they might wish to be free not to was never raised. Nor was every federal cultural institution suitably organized to respond to Pelletier's new policies quickly and well. Even in France decentralization had yet to prove itself; in Québec the democratization of the Quiet Revolution was still little more than rhetoric.

But Pelletier was a liberal democrat and an idealist, with little confidence in the capacity of the private sector to respond to cultural needs but strong confidence in the potential of the talented Canadian cultural community once it was backed by a generous government. And times had changed. Western thought had shifted from viewing culture as simply traditional "high culture" to a more inclusive notion embracing many ways of viewing reality, and many kinds of creative endeavour. It was no longer fashionable to look down on jazz or pop music, or on folk art, or on customized automobiles – all these things were now considered valid art. Indeed, McLuhan had suggested that all obsolete technologies become art, while the Dada movement had insisted that anything an artist says is art, is art.

116

The Department of the Secretary of State comprised three main branches, each with its own Assistant Under Secretary of State reporting to an Under Secretary of State (Jules Léger, at this time) who in turn was responsible to both the Secretary of State and the Minister without Portfolio responsible for Citizenship. The Arts and Culture Branch under André Fortier related to the various semi-autonomous cultural agencies and he was also seized with the heavy task of general departmental administration. Soon after his arrival, Fortier was instructed to begin drafting a mass of Cabinet memoranda to reflect the results of the consultations Pelletier and his staff had held with various cultural groups across the country. No subject matter escaped their attention, from crafts and museums to film and theatre, from cultural centres to publishing.

And the money flowed in and out. The Bilingualism Branch, as it came to be called, under Max Yalden, went out to sell the recommendations of the B&B to the provinces, the private and voluntary sectors, minority language groups and, indeed, to all Canadians. The branch even began to look at the value to the country of the federal dollars being transferred to the provinces for educational needs.

And the money flowed in and out. I was appointed Assistant Under Secretary of State for Citizenship shortly after Charles Lussier left for the Public Service Commission in January 1970. The Branch was supposed to develop and strengthen a sense of Canadian citizenship, chiefly through programs that would aid participation and assuage feelings of social injustice. Indian, Métis and Inuit political, social and cultural organizations were established and funded in the teeth of opposition from the Department of Indian Affairs; a women's bureau was set up before the government had commented on the Royal Commission's Report on the Status

117

of Women; Opportunities for Youth, travel and exchange and hostel programs were undertaken without the blessing of the Manpower, Welfare or Justice departments, and millions of dollars were made available to the Branch to ensure justice and fairness to every ethnic group that wished to preserve and celebrate its cultural heritage. A new Citizenship Act was brought forward so that landed immigrants regardless of sex could integrate more easily and quickly and with less discrimination than in the past; even extensive human rights legislation began to be drafted.

And the money flowed in and out. It was an exciting and rewarding time for the participants. The percentage of dollar increases was not excessive since the growth rate in expenditure for such programs was largely from a zero base. And then the government woke up – with the hangover of a minority administration – in 1972.

And the money flow dried up. Participation was dead; only the inelegant words democratization and decentralization remained and only in the policies of the National Museums of Canada. Gérard Pelletier resigned to become Minister of Communications; Jules Léger left to take up his post as Ambassador to Belgium; André Fortier moved to direct the Canada Council; Max Yalden was appointed Deputy Minister of Communications and at the end of 1973 I left to take over the National Museums of Canada. By that time the future role of the Department was beginning seriously to be questioned by the government itself.[2]

But much had been accomplished. Pelletier, when Secretary of State, had started allocating funds in 1968 to innovative programs that reached beyond traditional culture to help alleviate problems of unemployment and of social and political disadvantagement. Slowly, through the Cabinet process and backed by countless Cabinet memoranda, he, assisted by the stature, wisdom and

118

quiet effectiveness of his Under Secretary of State, Jules Léger, was convincing his political colleagues of the value of cultural activities and of the centrality of culture to the success of some of their departments' goals. A significant percentage of the projects funded under Opportunities for Youth and later under the Local Initiatives and New Horizons programs were cultural.

All this was in direct response to demand. Throughout the 1960s the lifestyles of Canadians had been changing dramatically. The very word lifestyle was novel in its suggestion that there could be more than one. Perhaps this was simply a development of capitalist prosperity. More and more people were managing their lives on a half-conscious principle of cost-benefit. Why make sacrifices in order to raise children who would in time consign their parents to the ash-can of history, as the present generation was consigning theirs? Why amass fortunes which could not be passed on to one's own posterity in any case? Some sought new visions of reality in drugs. Or opted out of the rat race to develop their capacity for pleasure. Many gave up the attempt to impress their neighbours by purchasing the symbols of affluence. Others dropped out of a school system which seemed capable of teaching them only the things they did not care to know.

Since the 1960s, the problem of technological unemployment had been recognized and discussed. Many Canadians had foreseen that as the problem grew with the advent of push-button factories and computerized accounting systems there would come a time when economic growth would fail to provide new jobs for those whom technology was putting out of work. They had predicted too that the solutions would be cultural ones. An ethic based on economic growth and work seemed to be dying. The cities were breeding a new generation; more than jobs and handouts, they wanted self-realiza-

119

tion and community. Many showed that their society could afford to feed them by living on the food thrown out by supermarkets. Instead of a stake in the economy and an abundance of consumer goods, many of them demanded recognition and participation and meaning in their lives. Pelletier's children were of this new generation and it was a large and vocal generation, often with its own political machinery and line into the mass media. The Canadian Conference of the Arts had declared a crisis in the arts in October 1968 and Pelletier, like Lamontagne before him, tried to respond to its criticisms and demands.

The Department of the Secretary of State became addicted to massive inquiries into one subject and another. Even the new structure for the National Museums was the cause of some friction in its first years, but the policy of democratization and decentralization was to lead to important programs of assistance to other Canadian museums. Funds for acquisitions were increased, although they are still negligible compared with the major French, American and Commonwealth museums and art galleries.

A new source of assistance for Canadian artists was the Art Bank, created in 1972 and administered by the Canada Council. A special appropriation of $5 million was provided to acquire, over five years, a bank of works by professional Canadian artists, which are available for leasing by government departments and agencies at a rental of 1 per cent of the cost of the work per month for display in government office and other buildings. In 1977-78, more than 8,000 works of over 900 artists had been acquired, and over 400 rental contracts placed with more than 80 departments and agencies in Canada and abroad. Another achievement was the passage of the Cultural Property Export and Import Control

Act, finally proclaimed in 1977, which seeks to prevent the dispersal of Canada's material cultural heritage.[3]

The Canadian publishing industry was the subject of increasing concern. An extraordinary piece of legislation in 1964 had extended tax deductions for advertising in Canadian magazines to the Canadian editions of *Time* and *Reader's Digest*, which together were taking in about 50 per cent of all the magazine advertising business in Canada. Worse still, in the fall of 1970, two of the largest and oldest publishing houses in Canada were sold to American firms. This led to the appointment of an Ontario Royal Commission on Publishing and to a provincial loan program to rescue McClelland and Stewart and other Canadian publishers from a similar fate. In 1976 an amendment to the federal Income Tax Act cancelled the tax deductions for advertising in the Canadian editions of *Time* and *Reader's Digest*.

Canadian magazines, which had been in decline since television drained off their advertising in the 1950s, began to be prosperous again: but this was a continental trend that had as much to do with the failing effectiveness of television advertising as with government regulation. The Secretary of State authorized an extensive study of the Canadian publishing industry in 1975; the report is still under review.

A feature of the late 1960s and 1970s had been the enormous increase in the cost of producing the performing arts, though government policies and dollars continued support on a scale much greater than for any other art form. The difficulty of negotiating with the unions concerned was aggravated by the notion that cultural institutions could recover their resultant losses from a supposedly bottomless public purse. Moreover, growth of the performing arts was stimulated by the erection at public cost of new auditoria and theatres. This movement

121

had begun in the late 1950s and early 1960s with new buildings or major additions to existing structures in Calgary and Edmonton, Vancouver, Toronto, Windsor, and Montréal. Several centennial projects of a similar kind produced significant capital investments in cultural activity centres in St. John's, Québec City, Charlottetown, Ottawa, Hamilton, Winnipeg, Regina and Saskatoon, as well as smaller theatres in Toronto, Edmonton and Calgary. The most lavish of all was the National Arts Centre in Ottawa, opened in 1969. With one or two exceptions, these houses across Canada attract audiences amounting to 70 per cent or more of capacity throughout the year. But all require subsidies which range consistently between 42 and 45 per cent of their operating costs. In the same period, the Québec government organized a system of *centres culturels*, on the French model, converting old premises and building new ones.

New buildings have helped new enterprises, all seeking and winning assistance from federal, provincial and municipal sources. Calgary and Edmonton now have theatre companies as good as those already established in other regions; the newest is Theatre London, while the Shaw Festival in Niagara-on-the-Lake is increasingly popular. Ottawa has a regular series of English- and French-language theatre productions. In Toronto alone there are some twenty-five experimental or avant-garde theatres producing mainly Canadian plays. The Centaur Theatre is at last providing Montrealers with acceptable English-language theatre. Feeding most of these companies with new talent is the National Theatre School in Montréal, which offers a complete training in all aspects of theatre in both official languages.

The Québec Opera, organized through the Place des Arts, has lapsed for want of financial controls, but there are now opera seasons in Vancouver and Edmonton, Calgary and Winnipeg, as well as those of the Cana-

122

dian Opera Company in Toronto and on tour, and the July Festival in Ottawa.

The three leading professional ballet companies have continued to flourish, and all have received international acclaim for performances abroad, while half a dozen or more modern dance companies are also tapping the available funds for the support of dance. The National Ballet School in Toronto, which provides bilingual academic education as well as ballet training, is one of only three or four of its class outside the Soviet Union.

While federal support for the arts was growing rapidly, even more in proportion was being spent by the provinces in certain areas. In the performing arts, for instance, between 1961 and 1971, provincial support increased by a factor of 10, from $0.5 to $5.0 million, while that of the Canada Council rose only by a factor of 7, from $1 to $6.9 million. Two aspects of this outpouring of public money for the arts should be noted. The first is that the "arts industry" employs thousands of Canadians in all parts of the country and has grown to a size and importance that deserves as much governmental attention and support as most other industries. The other more surprising aspect is that, at least in the case of performing companies, the money granted by governments is less than the amounts that flow back into general revenue. In a 1970-71 study of three major performing companies which together received $1.7 million in government grants, the Canada Council discovered that $2.2 million (or 127 per cent of the government contribution) was returned in direct and indirect taxes, while $2.8 million was paid out in salaries to 262 individuals and some $2.9 million went into the purchase of goods, materials and services to the general benefit of the economy. These telling figures do not seem to have had much impact on politicians.[4]

The other side of the coin shows that government

123

support for the arts is not only helping the arts industry but is also satisfying a widespread demand from citizens. The suggestion that more people go to high-culture events than to sporting events is not significant, since the real measure of interest is reflected in the vastly higher numbers of people who watch the latter on television. Yet actual attendance figures at high-culture events are impressive, and it is misleading to think in percentages in this context; 1 per cent of the population of Canada might not seem like much, but in reality it means nearly a quarter of a million citizens.

In 1972 a federal study of leisure activities was based on a sample of almost 50,000 representing what might be called the potential attendance – that is, the total civilian non-institutional population of Canada aged 14 and over, but excluding the Yukon and Northwest Territories, or about 13 million people.[5] The table on page 125 shows the numbers of people attending various kinds of events or places at least once in the three-month period covered by the study and the percentage of the potential attendance that they represent. Many attended more often than once, and the figures should not be totalled, for many of the same people are included in more than one group. The figures in the study are broken down by sex, age group, socio-economic level and region. An interesting feature is that in the first of the groups some 40 per cent were under twenty-five years of age, in the second about 43 per cent, and in the third some 60 per cent were under thirty-five.

True, statistics can nearly always be manipulated to prove any point, but the foregoing figures do represent a very large total attendance. Comparable figures for the United States estimate total audiences for major symphony orchestras at some 110 million, and for dance events at 15 million, with museum attendance at about 50 million (of whom, of course, a large proportion are

	Number* (000s)	% of potential
Live theatre	2,300	17.4
Classical music	1,380	10.4
Opera	460	3.5
Ballet	230	1.7
Art Galleries: (pay)	690	5.2
Art Galleries: (free)	690	5.2
Museums: (pay)	920	7.0
Museums: (free)	690	5.2
Historic Sites: (pay)	1,150	8.7
Historic Sites: (free)	1,150	8.7
Nonclassical music	2,990	22.6
Movies	8,000	60.9
Sporting events	5,290	40.0
Fairs, exhibitions	2,500	19.0
Other	2,500	19.0

* These are rough approximations, working back from percentages.

school children). In France, recent statistics reported by the ministry there reflect comparable numbers and increases in attendance figures. Without being too finicky about the actual numbers, it is evident that the number of people in Canada, as in most advanced industrial democracies, with a taste for even what some might call high culture of one sort or another represents a constituency that politicians can hardly afford to ignore.

But the growth in support of theatre, music or dance by governments and the public is part of a much broader development. For example, significant progress has been made in developing a Canadian film industry during the past decade. The Canadian Film Development Corporation has assisted or sponsored the production of feature films in Canada with some success, although there has been criticism of the Corporation's taste. The National Film Board has continued to win

125

more than its share of international awards, mostly for French-language feature films, documentaries and animated shorts. In 1976 a new tax measure allowed 100 per cent write-offs for investments in all-Canadian films; the result has been an enormous increase in investment. Extension of the 100 per cent write-off to co-productions has led to a great increase in foreign investment, but there has been dissatisfaction about the employment of foreign stars and inadequate Canadian content. An optimistic view is that "Canada finally has a national cinema ... films that express a recognizably Canadian sensibility and an industry capable of turning that sensibility into reality."[6] It is true that the international film-going public now appears to be judging Canadian films on their merits, but this is partly due to the calibre of some of the international stars appearing in them. There is still a long way to go. A comprehensive study of the problem was launched in 1975; the report, presented in April 1976, is still under consideration by the Secretary of State. But no one today can question the enormous increase in audiences at home and abroad that Canadian films enjoy, in spite of the most difficult problems of distribution.[7]

In broadcasting, the critical issue during the past decade was that of cablevision. The Canadian appetite for American programming is formidable. It has led, despite a suggested reluctance on the part of the CRTC, to more than half of all Canadian urban homes being equipped to receive American programming from stations in the United States, while both the CBC and the CTV networks include a high proportion of American programming in prime time. All cablevision undertakings are required to provide at least one channel for community programming, and several provinces argue that it would be more logical if community programming were regulated on the spot rather than by Ottawa.

But what do all these activities, or rather the resources set aside for them, add up to? Excluding the $17.6 billion Canadian governments spend on education, the first cultural rung on the ladder, any estimate of the amount of federal public funds assigned for "cultural" purposes must depend on how those purposes are defined. The 1978-79 Estimates of the federal government total over $46.5 billion. Of this amount, expenditure on the arts in general, film, broadcasting, libraries and archives, museums, and the performing arts amount to $738 million, or 1.59 per cent. Expenditures on UNESCO account for $5.1 million, and on citizenship and native peoples' cultural programs for $58.6 million, giving a total of 1.72 per cent. Broadening the definition of culture, the addition of expenditures on Official Languages ($254.7 million), education and training ($1,939 million), social and physical science research ($545 million), and recreation and sport ($227.1 million) results in a grand total of about $3.77 billion, or 8.11 per cent of all federal expenditure.

Concentrating, for the moment, on the more limited definition, we have a total figure of just over $802 million. But more than half of the total federal expenditure goes on such statutory items as social welfare services and support for post-secondary education. So it is more realistic to relate the cultural expenditures we are considering to the (non-statutory) voted portion of the total, or about $19,876 billion, of which they account for some 4 per cent. The ingredients of this total are best understood by a glance at the work and budgets of the federal departments and agencies concerned.

The Department of the Secretary of State, as we have seen, is supposed to be at the centre of federal support for the arts. The Arts and Culture Branch, after all, enjoys a budget of $16.5 million. The purpose of the Branch is "to provide advice and assistance to the Secretary of State in the formulation and development of

Federal Government Man-Years and Expenditures on Culture and Recreation

	1957/58		1967/68		1977/78		1978/79	
	MY's	$M	MY's	$M	MY's	$M	MY's	$M
Archives, galleries, theatres, etc.								
National Museums of Canada		0.5[b]	359	6.3	1,002	44.6	1,005	49.5
National Library		0.2	210	1.6	490	11.5	494	13.4
National Arts Centre Corp.		–	n/a	13.5	374	8.8	405	10.4
Admin. & Historical Branch Public Archives		0.5	268	2.0	408	11.4	414	13.0
		1.2	837	23.4	2,274	76.3	2,318	86.3
Parks, historic sites and other recreational areas								
Parks Canada, Indian Affairs & Northern Development		17.0	2,348	39.8	5,006	181.6	5,080	194.4

Film, radio and television

C.B.C.	12,487	522.4	11,793	467.0	9,035	144.0	36.1
National Film Board	963	34.1	963	28.9	749	8.8	3.8
Can. Radio - television & Telecomm. Commission	492	15.6	492	14.2	94	1.0[a]	
	13,942	572.1	13,248	510.1	843	153.8	39.9
Other culture and recreation							
Admin. Secretary of State	492	23.7	423	11.9	95	1.6	0.3
Arts & Culture, Sec. of State	50	16.5	43	11.2		–	–
Fitness & Amateur Sport, Nat. Health & Welfare	122	32.7	122	27.1	n.a.	5.0	–
Citizenship, Sec. of State	708	58.6	710	40.7	283	3.4	1.2[c]
Arts Support, Canada Council	301	34.9	301	35.9	n.a.	16.9	–[d]
	1,673	170.9	1,599	126.8	378	26.9	1.5
	23,013	1,023.7	22,127	894.8	4,406	243.9	59.6

a – Board of Broadcast Governors
b – National Gallery
c – Under Citizenship & Immigration
d – Operating funds provided by the income from a $53,000,000 endowment from the estates of Isaak Walton Killam and Sir James Dunn. Total income $2,368,000; expenditures $1,596,000.

policies and programs for the achievement of national arts and cultural objectives; to promote effective co-operation among the federal cultural agencies in the achievement of these objectives; to administer certain programs designed in support of these objectives, and to advise and assist the Government on matters of State protocol." The Assistant Under Secretary of State (Cultural Affairs and Education Support Branch) is responsible to the Under Secretary of State for the activities of some seventy officers and support staff. His terms of reference are broad and far-reaching but if he were to attempt seriously to carry them out the leaders of the cultural constituency in Canada and in the federal and provincial bureaucracies would probably effectively prevent his doing so. Nevertheless, the federal government has never permitted the Department of the Secretary of State and its Minister to be either the focus or co-ordinator of the vast number of cultural activities the government as a whole engages in, or of the resources voted for these activities.

The Department's legal advisers quaintly maintain that the Secretary of State is responsible for broadcasting policy in spite of the formal statements to the contrary in Bill C-24 tabled in the House of Commons. In fact, he is no more than the parliamentary spokesman for the CBC, with no powers of direction over it, though he must approve its estimates and assume full responsibility for the Corporation's conduct. The CBC has a budget of over $520 million, of which approximately half is assigned to the production and procurement of programs. The CBC is entitled to recall with pride that for thirty years or more, from the early days of radio to the establishment of the Canada Council in 1957, it was virtually the *only* source of public patronage for the arts, providing a livelihood for hundreds of Canadian authors, actors, composers, musicians and designers, in a period when live theatre was being extinguished, except in the largest commercial

130

centres, first by the movies and later by television. It has been said, with truth, that had there been no CBC there could have been no Stratford, for instance, because there would have been no pool of Canadian artists or audiences on which to draw.

It is still true today that the CBC, through its program budget, is by far the largest source of public support for artists in Canada. But this is not all; the CBC also sponsors talent festivals and competitions for composers, singers and instrumentalists, commissions special works from authors and composers, and produces public concerts for later or live broadcast diffusion. The CRTC, the regulatory body for all forms of telecommunication subject to federal legislative authority (including broadcasting), has a budget of $15.6 million; the parliamentary spokesman for the CRTC is the Minister of Communications, whose Department includes socio-cultural research programs with budgets on the order of $35 million.

The Canada Council, with a budget of $43.6 million "to promote the creation and enjoyment of works of art" is not subject to any form of ministerial direction. About 16 per cent of the arts budget is devoted to grants to individual artists, ranging from short-term grants of $600 a month to as much as $17,000 a year to "senior artists." Travel grants are available for artists. Arts organizations receive grants for special projects, but much of the Council's arts money goes for the support of the great national orchestras and ballet companies, the Canadian and other opera companies, theatre festivals, and the leading regional theatre companies. The need to support these national institutions is obvious, but there are critics who complain that this enshrinement of established performing organizations leaves too little money for experimental ventures, although these do indeed receive support on a scale greater than its critics appreciate.

The work of the Canada Council includes that of

131

the Canadian National Commission for UNESCO, with a budget of nearly $600,000. The Department of External Affairs budgets $4.5 million for UNESCO activities, and also contributes modestly, considering the opportunities, to the cost of sending Canadian performing arts companies, art exhibitions and publications to other countries. Though the details are hard to come by, there is some evidence that CIDA, too, is devoting dollars to cultural activity abroad.

A source of funds for painters and sculptors is the Department of Public Works, under the policy of allocating an additional one per cent to the cost of federal buildings for the purchase of works of art. On the capital budget of the department for 1978-79, this could amount to some $2.5 million but it is doubtful whether anything like that sum is spent annually for such purchases.

In addition to the Canada Council's grants to performing arts organizations, the Department of the Secretary of State made capital grants in 1977 amounting to $2.63 million under a special program "to help establish and maintain a national grid of performing arts facilities. ... Capital funding can be used for the construction or purchase of new facilities, or funding for associated capital equipment such as lighting, sound, seating, dressing rooms, curtains and air conditioning." In the wider sense of culture, the federal government spends some $58.6 million on citizenship and native people programs.

The National Film Board continues its successful career with total expenditures of $45.2 million, including $1.7 million for the Canadian Government Photo Centre. The Canadian Film Development Corporation, with a budget of some $4 million, carries on with its sponsorship of or financial participation in the production of Canadian feature films. The Film Festivals Bureau in the Department of the Secretary of State co-ordinated the

132

participation of 534 Canadian film entries in 108 film festivals around the world in 1976-1977; 54 of those festivals were competitive, and Canada won 66 awards.

The National Library has a budget of $13.4 million; a notable achievement in 1976 was the acquisition of the Jacob Lowy collection of rare books, one of the three most important Hebraic libraries in North America. The Public Archives, with a budget of $18.8 million, continues to grapple with the mushrooming volume of public records, including films, and has been more successful than it was a few years ago in retrieving important Canadian archival material from abroad.

The National Museums of Canada, incorporating the National Gallery, the National Museum of Man, the Canadian War Museum, the National Museum of Natural Sciences, the Museum of Science and Technology, and the National Aeronautical Collection has a budget of $49.5 million. Of this amount, $16.8 million is handled by the Programs Branch to assist designated museums and provide specialized services to all museums and their publics across Canada. When these cultural organizations and agencies were brought together under the Secretary of State in 1963-64, the Historic Sites Branch, a component of the National Parks organization, was forgotten. It is embedded in the Department of Indian Affairs and Northern Development with a budget of $46.2 million. Here again, the absence of a comprehensive policy dealing with our support of Canadian heritage leads to wasteful anomalies. In 1973 the federal government set aside a $12 million endowment fund for a new independent national institution, Heritage Canada, to enlist the participation of Canadians "in the important task of preserving the nation's historic and natural heritage."[7] And in the past two years the federal government has rediscovered July 1 as a national holiday. One result is that in 1978 it spent more than $4 million on the celebration, more than half of which went to performing artists.

The policy of providing sustaining grants and occasional capital to the voluntary sector has been maintained. Grants were made in 1976-77 of $42,000 to the Canadian Broadcasting League, $205,000 to the Canadian Conference of the Arts, and $70,000 to the Canadian Crafts Council. Outside Ottawa, institutions like the Fathers of Confederation Building Trust received $870,000; the Community Music School of Greater Vancouver, $111,111; and the Association for the Export of Canadian Books, $300,000; while a special grant of $600,000 was made to Newfoundland toward the celebration of its accession to Canada; all these added up to a total of about $2.2 million.

In 1977-78 the Department of Industry, Trade and Commerce budgeted for a contribution of $125,000 to the Montreal Book Fair, which was included in a total figure of about $800,000 for such objects as the improvement of Canadian industrial and fashion design. The Department of Supply and Services budgeted $3.4 million for the free distribution of federal government publications.

Two other responsibilities of the Secretary of State are worth mentioning here, though neither directly involves federal policy. The first is support for post-secondary education, involving statutory payments to the provinces totalling well over $1 billion (of the $17.6 billion mentioned earlier). The second is concerned with the promotion of bilingualism in Canadian society. These responsibilities include formula payments to the provinces toward the cost of second-language education, youth programs and special projects, with a total budget of $232.2 million for 1978-79. The office of the Commissioner of Official Language has a 1978-79 budget of $3.5 million.

134

To have a more complete picture of federal investment in cultural activities, we should note budgeted expenditures on research in the natural sciences by several departments and agencies totalling $1,386.7 million in 1978-79, in addition to approximately $180 million on Statistics Canada, $200 million on national parks and the National Capital Commission, and $35 million on fitness and amateur sport by the Department of National Health and Welfare.

So much for the billions of dollars and tens of thousands of bureaucrats the federal government provides in support of culture, however one wishes to define the word or its functions in government. It is time to look at the other level of government in our federation.

In the provinces, the movement toward organized attention to the arts, and later to culture more generally, began in Alberta and Saskatchewan in the 1940s, well in advance of either Québec or the federal government, and was followed by all the other provinces by the 1960s. But no province, even had it been so inclined, was in a position to match the resources, energy and pace shown by the federal government in these fields in the 1960s and 1970s. Nevertheless, total provincial expenditures on support for the arts and other cultural activities in 1977-78 are impressive, as shown in the following table. Although the figures are not identically based, where they have been made available from the provinces they do give a reasonable perspective on the relative amounts.

The provincial mechanisms for dealing with cultural activities, like the provinces themselves, show great variety. In Ontario, support is provided by the Department of Culture and Recreation, the Ontario Arts Council and, indirectly, the Ontario Educational Communications Authority, which operates TV Ontario; in addition, and uniquely, capital and non-capital grants are available

135

Provincial Expenditures on the
Culture and Recreation Function*

	1977/78 $M	1967/68 $M	1957/58 $M
Archives, galleries, theatres etc.			
British Columbia	9.0	1.0	0.5
Alberta	4.9	0.7	0.2
Saskatchewan	7.4	0.8	0.3
Manitoba	2.2	0.3	0.2
Ontario	33.6	9.9	1.1
Quebec	28.2	6.5	2.3
Prince Edward Island	1.0	0.2	0.1
New Brunswick	4.2	0.8	0.2
Nova Scotia	4.9	0.9	0.3
Newfoundland	1.9	0.5	0.2
	97.3	21.6	5.4
Parks, historic sites & other recreational areas			
British Columbia	35.2	5.0	2.5
Alberta	57.3	5.4	1.4
Saskatchewan	3.1	2.1	0.5
Manitoba	15.2	1.8	0.4
Ontario	72.3	8.2	4.7
Quebec	94.9	11.6	3.4
Prince Edward Island	4.0	0.1	0.1
New Brunswick	1.8	0.9	0.1
Nova Scotia	0.8	0.8	–
Newfoundland	3.5	1.2	0.3
	288.1	37.1	13.4

* Estimates, presentations and disclosures were inconsistent and in many instances objective descriptions rather vague. Consequently a considerable amount of individual judgement had to be exercised assembling these figures.

136

Film, radio & television

British Columbia	0.6	–	–
Alberta	2.2	0.2	0.1
Saskatchewan	0.1	0.2	0.2
Manitoba	0.8	–	–
Ontario	14.3	3.1	0.2
Quebec	5.0	1.5	–
Prince Edward Island	–	–	–
New Brunswick	–	–	–
Nova Scotia	0.6	0.1	0.1
Newfoundland	–	–	–
	23.6	5.1	0.6

Other culture and recreation

British Columbia	12.4	1.8	0.1
Alberta	4.0	1.8	–
Saskatchewan	6.4	0.7	0.1
Manitoba	8.5	2.1	–
Ontario	99.0	2.5	0.6
Quebec	69.3	5.2	0.2
Prince Edward Island	0.2	0.2	–
New Brunswick	1.9	1.1	–
Nova Scotia	5.5	1.0	–
Newfoundland	9.7	1.2	0.2
	216.9	17.6	1.2
	625.9	81.4	20.6
% of total estimates	1.6	1.0	1.0

from the profits of the Wintario lottery. In Manitoba, the instruments for support are the Department of Tourism, Recreation and Cultural Affairs, and the Manitoba Arts Council. Saskatchewan has a similar arrangement with its Department of Culture and Youth, and the pioneering Arts Board; as a result perhaps of its diffuse demography, there is a peculiarly down-to-earth approach, for instance in the unique emphasis on crafts as well as the arts, and the province is active in promoting co-operatively owned community cablevision systems. Alberta Culture, the successor to, first, a Cultural Development Branch under the Provincial Secretary and, later, a Department of Culture, Youth and Recreation, administers some of the most enlightened cultural legislation in Canada, which encompasses a program of matching grants, in varying proportions, to all corporate and private contributions. New Brunswick, which has declared English and French its official languages, has a Cultural Affairs Branch in its Department of Youth. Cultural support is provided in Nova Scotia by the Department of Recreation. All these provinces provide support, in various ways and different proportions, to arts institutions and organizations, community and other arts groups, ethno-cultural organizations, festivals and special projects, as well as individual grants and scholarships. Ontario, Manitoba, Saskatchewan and British Columbia support publishing undertakings and, along with Nova Scotia, have funds for provincial art banks or individual purchases of works in the visual arts. Several provinces now support artists-in-residence programs in universities and community colleges.

Cultural support activities in the three remaining English-language provinces are less comprehensive. The British Columbia Cultural Fund, administered by the Cultural Services Branch of the Department of Recreation and Conservation, is the source of per capita grants to qualifying community arts councils, and of scholarships and fellowships tenable at "recognized and advanced schools of specific cultural disciplines"; funds are not available for basic workshops, short-term grants, or grants to individual artists. Newfoundland has a Cultural Affairs Division in its Department of Tourism, but most cultural planning and promotion is routed through Arts and Cultural centres in St. John's and four other com-

138

munities, on similar lines to the centres culturels in Québec. In Prince Edward Island, although no formal action has been taken, a minister is designated to look after cultural affairs; most arts activities are processed through the Fathers of Confederation Buildings Trust, which operates the Charlottetown Arts Centre, a special Centennial project substantially supported by the federal government.

In sum, the people of Canada today are pouring out treasure through both provincial and federal levels of government – and they are the same tax supporters of each jurisdiction – on a scale greater than at any other time in our history. They are doing it in ways that even governments and parliaments should be prepared to concern themselves with rather more than they do. Certainly the audiences, clients and cultural clergy should. I shall return to that subject. It may be noted that the one province omitted from this chapter's discussion was Québec. Embedded in a country and a sub-continent dominated by United States' cultural activities, by the English language, by Canadian federal and non-French provincial treasuries, how has Québec coped in recent years with its advancing cultural revolution?

Confederation is a compact, made originally by four provinces but adhered to by all the nine provinces who have entered it, and I submit . . . that this compact should not be lightly altered.

                                   Sir Wilfrid Laurier, 1907.

The supremely important task of our artists and writers is to retain a distinct French life and soul and daily to increase its power.

                                   Canon Lionel Groulx, 1918.

You in Canada should not be dependent either on the United States or on Great Britain. You should have your own films and exchange them with those of other countries. You can make them just as well in Toronto as in New York City.

                                   D. W. Griffith, 1925.

History is the most dangerous product ever invented by the chemistry of the mind. . . . It makes one dream, it intoxicates the people, it leads them to give birth to counterfeit memories, it exaggerates their reflexes, it perpetuates their old wounds, it torments them when they rest, it drives them to megalomania or paranoia. It makes nations bitter, arrogant, insufferable and vain.

                                   Paul Valéry, 1930.

We carry in our very bones the mind and marrow of our forebears. No, a nation cannot separate itself from its past any more than a river can separate itself from its source, or sap from the soil whence it arises.

                                   Canon Lionel Groulx, 1937.

I like to think that subconscious Canada is even more important than conscious Canada and that there is growing up swiftly in this country, under the surface, the sense of a great future and of a great separate destiny – as Canada.

                                   John Grierson, 1947.

SIX

The Québec Department of Cultural Affairs was established in 1960, and a chain of *centres culturels* was developed throughout the province. The 1967-68 departmental budget of $12.2 million grew to $42.8 million within a decade – a great deal of money by any standard of comparison. But if you are a Québécois, perceiving yourself as a member of a majority culture threatened first by a Canadian (anglophone) cultural intrusion on which more than a billion dollars is being lavished, and secondly by the inevitable overflow from American cultural institutions, the Québec departmental expenditures assume a different image.

The impact of the Quiet Revolution on Québec cultural development helped to increase awareness of needs and of the immense task still to be accomplished. In addition, the growing Québec cultural bureaucracy was casting envious eyes upon what seemed to them the systematic, efficient way in which culture was being structured by Ottawa. The transfer of cultural agencies to the Secretary of State Department in the general reorganization of 1963, making the department a clearer focus for federal cultural activities and policy, did not go unnoticed in Québec City. As the federal Minister and his Department began to take a closer look at the uses to be made of film and broadcasting, they were publicly discussing cultural areas in which Québec not only felt especially weak or vulnerable but in which it too wanted to move but not against so powerful a competitor. The CBC and the NFB were seen as becoming increasingly identified with Québécois as well as with Canadian culture; and there was a real concern in the Department of Cultural Affairs over the possibility of being outdistanced by Ottawa. The preparation of the provincial White Paper of 1965 was the result of feelings of impotence, anger and despair.

The Minister of Cultural Affairs, Pierre Laporte, was willing to accept what was perceived in his ministry as the challenge from Ottawa. A working group was formed under the direction of Guy Frégault. On January 20, 1965, Pierre Laporte announced that the White Paper would constitute "the very basis of cultural policy in Québec, since we realize that such a policy is needed to avoid a lot of wasted energy." The Provincial Arts Council, which was still without a constitution, was to play an advisory role. Guy Frégault had few kind words to say about the Council: "Like the political class, the Provincial Arts Council was comprised of eminent persons. Like all such groups, it was well-informed but basically conservative. In its view we were going overboard in affirming the national character of Québec, and the Council reminded us that Québec was only a province." Jean-Charles Falardeau, one of these "eminent persons," and President of the Council, sadly commented on this period: "There is so much that could be said, especially about our not having had the sense to discover America at the right time!" But at the time, he reserved his remarks for his employers.

The White Paper being prepared was to be a policy document outlining the "national" objectives of a cultural policy for Québec. For the first time since Confederation the cultural role of the provincial government would be openly and clearly stated: "What is actually being discussed is the preservation, from a dynamic viewpoint, of a cultural identity, and this can be accomplished only by a government with which the people can identify fully – namely the government of Québec."

This was the new Québec's reply to the Massey Report after the Report of the Tremblay Commission set up by Duplessis remained, if not secret, at least unproductive where its main recommendations were concerned. In 1964-65 the federal government's expenditures on culture and especially on the Canada Council, while a source of concern to those who cared in Québec, were not a source of fear. Guy Frégault was able to comment: "The federal contender did not appear to have the muscles of an unbeatable champion." But by the time of Expo 67 the federal government was spending millions more on culture and by the mid-seventies the budget of the Canada Council had tens of millions more than during its initial years. Guy Frégault concluded that, "By the end of a decade the humble federal competitor of the mid-sixties had become king of the castle." It appeared to the Québec bureaucracy, intellectual elite and nationalist politicians that what was taking place was a race against time. It is one of the great tragedies of my generation that in an issue so central to the meaning, potential and viability of our federation, the ad hoc and largely unconscious federal support of culture in response to Canadian demands, a response that came in fits and starts, should have been viewed in an important and culturally unique part of this country as a preconceived plot against the attempt of a minority group whose ancestors helped found Canada to preserve their spiritual integrity.

Language was also one of the main concerns expressed in Pierre Laporte's draft White Paper. And while it contained what appears today to be a mild reference to "the priority language of Québec," it also made clear that the duty of the province was to defend multiculturalism and promote the distribution of "works produced by members of the large Anglo-Saxon minority and by members of all of Québec's ethnic groups." The authors of the White Paper expressed a desire to see the integration of existing services with the Ministry of Cultural Affairs in the interest of promoting coherent action. For example, they wanted the jurisdiction of the department extended to cinema. The White Paper contained sixty recommendations touching all areas of artistic endeavour. Incredibly, to the outside world at least, it was never tabled in the National Assembly and was not made public until 1976 by another Liberal minister, Jean-Paul L'Allier. For, in the provincial elections of June 1966, the Liberals were defeated and Daniel Johnson became the Union Nationale Premier of Québec.

He appointed Jean-Noël Tremblay as his Minister of Cultural Affairs. Tremblay's personality as well as his politics were rather different from those of his predecessors. He was, if anything, a more sensitive and cultivated individual, with a strong pragmatic bent, less inclined to make purely partisan policies in the field of culture. He found Frégault an excellent administrator, though uncongenial, and when, at his request, the leader removed this Deputy to a new post, Tremblay replaced him with a liberal economist from Sherbrooke University, Raymond Morrissette.[1] The new Deputy was asked to prepare a comprehensive policy to be carried out by a suitably restructured department. Tremblay did not really reject Laporte's White Paper, for on assuming office he discovered about a dozen drafts of it, "no less than thirteen versions" he told me. The final draft, still lacking Cabinet approval, contained marginalia in the hand of former Premier Lesage, warning against the political dangers of some of Laporte's proposals.

And Tremblay had his own ideas about cultural policy. He at once made it clear that the previous government's policy, as he stated, "... does not represent the policy of the new government" (*Le Devoir*, September 21, 1966). Although he succeeded in increasing provincial grants to cultural groups from $3.2 to $5 million in his first budget, he knew that the previous administration had raised hopes and expectations in the Québec cultural community which could not possibly be financed in the short run. He set about creating the "instruments de la culture" which were intended to meet long-term needs. Some of these were allowed to lapse by his successors, but he succeeded in establishing others that survived his term of office. He established the National Library of Québec and set in motion the reorganization of regional museums under a director general, launched the Grand Théâtre de Québec and the magazine *Culture Vivante* and extended the province's cultural facilities through fifty-five new cultural centres in cities like Rimouski, Trois-Rivières, Chicoutimi and Beauceville as well as Québec City and Montréal.

In a brief memoir communicated to me personally, Tremblay recalls the part he played in all these initiatives, stressing his concern with decentralization as well as with the pursuit of excellence. Not unnaturally, he regrets the demise of several imaginative projects he initiated, including the Québec Opera and L'Institut national de la Civilisation, as well as the floating exhibition which was to carry displays of Québec culture to some thirty ports in Ontario, the Maritimes and even Louisiana. To the accusation of elitism, he replies, "What one must avoid, in my opinion, is the levelling and reduction of all human activities to the lowest common denominator."

Tremblay was different in one important respect from his predecessors: he was an unqualified nationalist who did not mince words or fudge sentences. He was charged publicly from time to time with being a separatist. He believed firmly in the indivisible trinity of education, language and culture and categorically refused to "allow the federal government to take any initiatives in such a vital area." His views were clear. He called upon Ottawa "to turn over to the Québec Government, with no strings attached, sufficient capital to enable the latter to establish its plan of action and to assist cultural organizations in accordance with a coherent, carefully planned policy" (*Le Devoir*, August 8, 1966), and accused the federal government of "economic imperialism." His public declarations on the French language and its connection with immigration policy were to echo across the country for almost a decade (*Le Devoir*, November 15, 1966). Toward the end of his term as minister, he delivered an address at Scarborough College in Toronto bitterly denouncing what he believed to be federal interference in provincial cultural matters that touch on education and culture. His words have been made familiar through more recent spokesmen of similar views.

As far as we are concerned, this is a hindrance, an unequal partnership, a duplication of efforts and a situation where one government is trying to outdo the other; this is particularly evident in the area of culture. Personally, I know that if it were possible for me to obtain the money that Ottawa spends on culture in Québec, I could easily implement a coherent cultural policy on exchanges and relations with the governments of the other member states of Confederation (*Le Devoir*, February 5, 1969).

Where he differed most from his predecessors and indeed his successors to the Cultural portfolio was less in the actual views he held than in his openness in sharing them with Canadians. Like his leader, he was never a Trojan horse.

It is well to recall the atmosphere of the time. Students of the Quiet Revolution had interpreted Expo as a product of the new spirit of optimism in Québec, another step toward putting Québec on the world map and making waves in Canada as a whole. Nineteen sixty-seven was also the year of General de Gaulle's "Vive le Québec libre!", a year in which France, having deserted her colony and compatriots two centuries earlier, returned gloriously along the Chemin du Roy. The Parti Québécois, headed by René Lévesque, was founded in 1968. When the federal elections came, Québécois' votes were captured en masse by Pierre Elliott Trudeau with his appeal for a more "just society." In 1968 Québécois were intensely aware of the duality of their French-Canadian identity. Trudeau, Pelletier and Marchand, three of their own, were in Ottawa and the people of the Province took pride in what English-speaking Canadians called "French power."

But for Québec the real problems of cultural evolution remained within the power of their provincial bureaucracy and political machinery. During the preparation of Pierre Laporte's draft White Paper, there had been an appreciation of the importance of education to the protection of Québec's culture and people. The Commission of Inquiry on the teaching of the arts in Québec produced its report in 1968.[2] It is generally agreed that the report was a work of exceptional quality. However, like the draft White Paper of 1965, its main proposals remained largely on the shelf. The Commission, presided over by Professor Marcel Rioux, carried out extensive consultations among those associated with the arts and formulated concrete proposals on the specific subject of the teaching of the arts as well as on general matters of cultural reform. The Rioux Report was based on the principle that under a new system of education, artistic training must occupy a far more significant place than in the past: "Society must provide people with the means to adapt to the period in which they live and to find collective answers to all of the great challenges presented by a technological society." Education was a key factor in this search for answers in the sixties, but the mood was changing.

In his book *Le Temps des otages*, Jean Paré refers to the period immediately following, between 1970 and 1976, as a time "in parentheses." It was a time of gestation and development in the midst of what appeared to be unstable if not chaotic circumstances. First came the October crisis in 1970, followed in the next six years by a succession of seemingly interminable strikes which paralysed important sectors of the community.

The year 1976 brought Mayor Drapeau's promised Olympic Games, leaving Canadians, but especially Québécois, with a large bill. While some economists were saying that Québec was experiencing a crisis of industrial growth, the pace of economic development seemed to others to have thrust what was left of a rural society into a state of urban confusion. Québec Hydro and the Caisses populaires Desjardins were the material symbols of the change. The gigantic James Bay power development project was brought into being while fundamental conflicts over ecology and ethnology were aggravated by the apparent unpreparedness of members of an uneasy and concerned citizenry. There was an acceleration of

148

industrial expansion in spite of this uneasiness; in spite of the capital costs, nuclear power plants and asbestos mines were planned or initiated. At the same time the province entered a new era of scandals revealed by the Commission d'enquête sur le crime organisé (CECO). The tainted meat scandal led to public investigations that traced its ramifications to the very rich and influential. Montréal began to be referred to as a "disaster zone" and the shift of money, professionals, and influential financiers and commercial entrepreneurs to Ontario and the United States that had had a slow beginning in the fifties and sixties now dramatically accelerated.

But the decade was not all doom and gloom. For some, like sociologist Marcel Rioux, it was a "new stage of development in Québec society." Gradual but marked changes were occurring in group attitudes. Major changes were also taking place in the sensitivities and mood of Québécois, a process which had started during the Quiet Revolution and earlier. The struggle to surmount its problems enabled Québec society not only to mature and rationalize its political directions but also to become more open and future-oriented. The new society was inextricably linked to the new culture; one reflected and was dependent upon the other. The concept of heritage acquired a new dimension, representing the influences of the past, the reality of the present and the hope of the future; it filtered down to street level and into people's homes. Being a Québécois was also linked with the future. Québec culture would henceforth be rooted in the foundations of Québec francophone society, accepting and facing problems instead of either sweeping them under the rug or tolerating a leadership that handed over their souls to Rome and their bodies to Wall Street. So went the rhetoric. A new generation of artists, musicians, singers, poets was everywhere expressing a new national-ist optimism. The theatre and novels bore witness in a vital way to these changes in society, and more than ever popular singers had become the voice of a formerly silent majority.

During this time, the Department of Cultural Affairs, with its customary personnel and budgetary shortages, was trying, if not to lead, at least to be seen to be a part of this changing society. Guy Frégault was twice Deputy Minister of Cultural Affairs, from 1962 to 1968 and from 1970 until 1975. When he left the department in September 1975 he submitted to his Liberal minister Jean-Paul L'Allier an analysis of the Québec cultural situation as he saw it. The department had been in existence fifteen years. Frégault began by mentioning the fact that the stimulus for its creation had been the Massey Report:

> In creating the Department of Cultural Affairs, Québec brought to an end a virtual federal monopoly on its own territory and placed cultural affairs among the matters which in terms of administration, normally fall within the public domain. In other words, in 1961 Québec itself finally became the agent of cultural development.

But the progress had been slow and intermittent. Frégault was frustrated and the cause of these frustrations was, of course, the shortage of funds and the lack of Cabinet attention. In addition, there was a question concerning the range of the Department's activities, since its jurisdiction included numerous areas of activity not normally associated with cultural development. For the Deputy Minister, a cultural policy had to be global and well co-ordinated at its base, developed on the basis of consultations with its clients and implemented with the participation of the general citizenry. But, according to Frégault, the Department of Cultural Affairs already was

150

out of touch with the Québec cultural milieu. In fact, what Frégault was warning his Minister of was that after fifteen years the Department had failed. He was saying to L'Allier what Tremblay had already said to him.

Outside the Department there were growing voices in support of this contention. In 1975 a group of people from the Québec film industry decided to occupy the premises of the Cinema Supervisory Board in order to force the Québec government into passing legislation to protect and stimulate the development of Québec cinema. This broadly supported gesture was one demonstration of the dissatisfaction that existed with the performance of the Department of Cultural Affairs. A research group on cultural sovereignty was formed to set up a Cultural Tribunal to hear testimony from anyone who had something to say about the activities of the Department.

The Tribunal, presided over by Marcel Rioux, held hearings across the province in order to determine the most effective means of countering what it regarded as the massive invasion by United States (and English-Canadian) culture and to devise a global plan for cultural development. The Cultural Tribunal's report began by mentioning the fact that in Québec, the cultural policies of the federal government were more generous with regard to Québec's cultural agencies and artists than those of the Québec government; it quoted an assessment made by the then minister, Denis Hardy: "Cultural sovereignty implies searching for the cultural identity of Québec, safeguarding this identity in an English-speaking cultural context and establishing within the Government of Québec the judicial and financial powers required for its further development." The Rioux Report, like earlier investigations and studies, was one more indication of Québec's increasing desire to have its cultural institutions more responsive to its growing needs.[3]

If Québec's cultural industries *were* being overwhelmed by a flood of cultural products from foreign countries, what measures had been or could be adopted by Québec to protect them? Québec's recording industry, film industry, periodical, paperback and comic-strip publishing houses were all victims of "dumping." People involved in these industries testified before the Tribunal about their ineffectual efforts to preserve their businesses in the face of giant multinationals, especially those of France and the United States. Culture was something that involved all Québécois, representing as it did "the signs, behaviour models and even the rules which enable a society to recognize and define itself." Culture was "a way of living and communicating"; and Québec's culture was being constantly assailed by foreign cultures. This situation posed a threat to Québec's existence as a people. Cultural sovereignty, like economic independence, had to march hand in hand: "The less sovereignty a people has, the lower its standard of living will be."

The intention of the members of the film industry when they occupied the offices of the Cinema Supervisory Board was to obtain legislation to assist Québec cinema. On August 5, 1975, Denis Hardy was transferred from the Ministry of Cultural Affairs to the Department of Communications. He carried with him the responsibility for cinema, including Bill 1, which had been assented to on June 19, 1975. Bill 1 recommended the establishment of L'Institut québécois du cinéma, and the replacement of L'Office du Film du Québec, by the Direction générale du Cinéma et de l"Audio-visuel (Cinema and Audio-Visual Branch – CAVB). It also provided for special financial, tax and legal benefits to assist more rapid development of the industry in Québec. After some difficulty and delay, the Québec Cinema Institute was able to form its Board of Directors, and the CAVB finally found a director. The Québec Cinema Institute is an independent agency consisting of seven members appointed by the Lieutenant-Governor-in-Council. The members report directly to the Minister of Communications. The Institute's initial budget, in 1977, was $4.9 million for cinema and audio-visual productions. Its role is equivalent to that of the Canadian Film Development Corporation and it is responsible for promotion of cinema in Québec. The CAVB co-ordinates government production and sponsorship in Québec, as a division of the Department of Communications. Bill I on the cinema is currently being revised to further strengthen the film industry in the province.

The Québec Department of Communications also houses the Office de Radio-télédiffusion du Québec, called Radio-Québec. When Jean-Paul L'Allier was Minister of Communications he requested the preparation of a Yellow Paper on Radio-Québec, a report and synthesis of memoranda submitted during a process of regional consultations across Québec. One result was that Radio-Québec has become more regionalized in its productions and has been granted an increasingly important role in the broadcasting of cultural material throughout Québec.

When he began his duties with the Department of Cultural Affairs in August 1975, L'Allier was faced with a challenge the magnitude of which had grown with each of his predecessors. The Québec Department of Cultural Affairs had always been a marginal Department in budgetary terms. L'Allier produced a Green Paper stating: "Cultural Affairs, a marginal department, has with the passage of time become alienated from the outside world. It seems to have gradually refrained from intervening. ... " His Green Paper was an attempt to rekindle the cultural flame. Entitled *Pour l'évolution de la politique culturelle*, it was published in the spring of 1976. Taking into account the increasing cultural momentum of the seventies, L'Allier wished to provide Québec with the means to derive maximum benefit from provincially supported activities. The paper was well received by members of the artistic community in Québec, who commented on it and offered suggestions to improve it. It proposed giving the arts in Québec the increased support which artists themselves saw as indispensable to the development of their community's culture, and at the same time giving culture a mission of "creating an environment."

L'Allier proposed a policy of "cultural nationalism," a term he preferred to "cultural sovereignty," making Québec the sole author of its policies and the ultimate decision-making centre. Suggesting that Québec revamp its cultural policies and create a number of cultural budgets, he berated the Province for its inertia and its lack of structured, forceful cultural institutions under provincial authority, in comparison with the vigorous policy of the federal government in Québec, which he and his advisers perceived naïvely as being directed by a highly structured institution. The Green Paper, largely the work of his predecessors Tremblay, Laporte and their respective deputy ministers, proposed the creation of two key agencies: the Régie du patrimoine (Heritage Bureau) and the Conseil de la culture. The Heritage Bureau, a "quasi-judicial tribunal operating autonomously," would possess "the sole responsibility for deciding on the recognition, classification or other matters affecting the status of cultural property." In addition, the establishment of regional property commissions was recommended for each of Québec's ten administrative regions. Their essential function would be to advise the Heritage Bureau. The Cultural Council, a "decision-making agency having an executory function in relation to the public resources set aside for the protection and promotion of Québec culture, shall also be a structure for cultural consultation, participation and education." The Cultural Council would be autonomous. There would also be regional councils to advise the minister and the cultural Council.

The Green Paper envisaged the Department of Cultural Affairs as a service department, emphasizing "cultural orchestration, distribution and accessibility" and functioning as "an intermediary department in relation to the other departments." The revitalized Department would also be responsible for drafting policies to protect and promote Québec's cultural industries, in film, records, publications and so on. However, "the Cultural Council shall have the primary responsibility for administering and developing Québec's policies to assist artists in their work." The Council would thus be responsible for the administration of grants. By and large it was the parallel to proven federal structures and institutions.

As far as museum activities were concerned, the Green Paper recommended the creation of a Québec Museums Commission, composed mainly of Québécois other than civil servants, which would be responsible for the general supervision of the museums' operations. There was also seen to be a need for a Québec museum of arts and popular traditions and for a public museums network. The document also proposed cultural exchanges with the other provinces and with other parts of the French-speaking world; "In order to reach its full potential, Québec's cultural policy must make provision for each of Canada's ten provinces. ... We must also endeavour to carry out more exchanges with Ontario and the other provinces in which there are large groups of French Canadians." Again, partly as a consequence of the assistance of federal officials from the National Museums of Canada, the proposal was largely one to establish a provincial counterpart to an existing federal institution.

The Green Paper was intended mainly as a basis

155

for discussion among Québec's professional cultural groups and with the interested public. And it was not unrelated to L'Allier's personal political game plan. In the years I had known him, he was always successful in combining his broad intelligence with his narrow ambitions. Meetings, debates and information sessions were organized, and comments and further suggestions were made in all of Québec's newspapers. The Green Paper had at least succeeded in bringing about closer relations between the Department and the clients it had been established to serve. It was the summation of a decade of reports and rhetoric and frustration.

Then came the provincial elections and a new party government on November 15, 1976. When the independentist Parti Québécois came to power it initially expressed its agreement in principle with most of the recommendations in L'Allier's Green Paper. Soon after, the picture changed. Apparently some of the new separatist ministers feared the creation of a number of semi-autonomous agencies within the Ministry of Cultural Affairs.

However, when the new administration came down to the wire and had to face up to the need to gain approval for the allocation of funds in the National Assembly, Québec's cultural institutions did, in fact, receive budget increases. The amount voted for the Office de la langue française, the function and purpose of which were expanded, rose from $5.8 million to $7.4 million, an increase of nearly 27 per cent. The budget for the Department of Cultural Affairs rose from $45,586,900 to $57,103,200, up nearly 30 per cent. The Department of Communications, which includes the Québec Broadcasting Bureau and the Cinema and Audio-Visual Branch, was voted $78,119,200, a rise of slightly more than 7 per cent over the previous year's $72,936,800. The additional financial resources allocated to the Department of Cul-

156

tural Affairs were intended not only to cover a 10.5 per cent increase in staff from 869 to 960, but also to ensure a number of other advances, including improvements at the Musée du Québec, the further development of central lending libraries, assistance to private and public museums, regional tours by theatre, music and dance companies, and the conservation of cultural property.

Earlier in 1972 the Office de la langue française had become a part of the Department of Education; on July 22, 1974, a law was passed making it an independent body linked to the Executive Council. From 1974 to August 26, 1977, it was called la Régie de la langue française. On August 26, 1977, when Bill 101 was passed, describing the regulations governing language use in Québec, the Régie once again became the Office de la langue française, linked administratively to the Executive Council and represented by the Minister of State for Cultural Development, Camille Laurin. During the 1976 -77 "information" campaign, the issue of language was still paramount and the following slogan used widely; "De plus en plus au Québec, c'est en français que ça s'passe."

On August 18, 1977, the minister responsible to Laurin for dealing with short-term and operational cultural matters, Louis O'Neill, gave his blessing to the idea of regional cultural councils. In doing so he stressed the function of these councils, namely "to advise the department on regional cultural situations, on the needs of the people in the regions and on their objectives in so far as cultural development is concerned." The regional cultural councils are in touch with the regional offices of the Department of Cultural Affairs and receive their operating budgets from the Department.

On assuming power, the new government decided to reorganize the previous Cabinet system and establish super-ministries of state. The cultural Ministry was one of

157

those. The Ministry set about preparing yet another White Paper on culture in Québec, a comprehensive, global study of Québec's cultural needs, to include proposals on education, the environment, science, arts, communications and almost any subject the authors felt were encompassed within their definition of culture. Laurin named as leader of the group drafting the document, the conservative radical sociologist Fernand Dumont, his friend and ally in the drafting and strategy associated with the controversial language Bill 101. Dumont stated publicly that he intended to treat the study broadly so that even the subjects of alcoholism, housing, obesity, ageing, smoking and drug abuse would not be omitted.

Part of Dumont's mandate was to deal with inequities caused by age, sex, income and particularly the plight of minorities in Québec which a home-grown cultural policy might help reduce. Dumont had a pretty clear idea of what he wished to say before he started and a few months after his appointment leaks and various drafts of his paper began to appear. In an early, unpublished draft of his study there is an examination of ways to change the current state of affairs: "The official and often the actual image of the various ethnic minorities is that they should be lumped together with the English-speaking culture." The main means of effecting a change, the author suggested, would be to promote dialogue between the "French-speaking majority" and newly arrived immigrants, by means of a "policy of receptiveness" which is virtually non-existent today. Communication would be established mainly through the media, especially radio and television. The government would supervise the implementation of a "basic French-language service" to provide everybody with access to French-language culture. Heavy concentrations of English-speakers might also have access to the media for their own cultural expression. Finally, ethnic groups could be given air time for the same purpose. Radio-Québec would play a key role in this, both as regards the learning of French, and exposure to the culture of Québec and of the various ethnic groups: "The objective of Radio-Québec is to give Québec back to the Québécois. Québec is also composed of minorities, and Radio-Québec will be more attentive to this audience in its programming."

In addition, another draft paper that fell into my hands recommended the creation of a Conseil Supérieur des Communications, which would include representatives from the ethnic minorities. The principle, long recognized by earlier Québec administrations (and by the federal government), that minorities make up an integral part of the culture in Québec as elsewhere was clearly stated: "There is no such thing as a culture that contains no minorities." And the commitment is made to carry on a genuine dialogue with the English-speaking minority, which already has a strong network of institutions, especially in the Montréal region. Rather than constituting a separate sector in the cultural policy, the minorities were viewed in this particular draft as part of Québec culture and the recommendations of the authors to the government states: "The prolific contributions made by its minority groups must be seen as a welcome addition to Québec culture as such." In order to avoid assimilation of the minorities, the Québec government would be asked to devise a policy of cultural exchanges within Québec. This would be planned to permeate all sectors of social life, including, among others, the Québec public service, the educational establishment, the media and so on.

With regard to its native peoples, the intellectuals advising the Parti Québécois did not consider them a minority and their draft promotes the policy to offer

159

natives "full political sovereignty in certain territories."
Once this has occurred, "it is hoped that the co-operation
agreements concluded between the two sovereign part-
ners will lead to a genuine cultural interpenetration."

But the various drafts I obtained were altered
many times before the document was tabled in the Assembly and its recommendations presumably will be altered or adjusted before it becomes law, if it, or any part
of it, ever does become operative. Indeed, in an article in
Maclean's magazine published in March 1978, David
Thomas, the magazine's Québec correspondent, suggests
that the document he had seen before the official version
was released "even treads on the sensitive area of compulsory assimilation of Québec's minority groups into the
mainstream of French society." Perhaps this should be
read as evidence of anglophone anxiety generated by Bill
101.[4] Even the early drafts I had seen did not go that far.

Thomas reported his extensive interviews with
Dumont and Laurin, expressing alarm at the extent of
state control he believed they were likely to propose.
"Communications, labour relations, housing and health,
as well as the obvious domains of entertainment and the
arts," he notes, "are treated as deserving direct government control and guidance." According to Thomas, the
White Paper for Laurin is to be "Québec's Declaration of
Independence." Of particular interest is Dumont's remark, "I have always considered a collective project as
something mainly cultural. The economy is not an end in
itself: culture is."

Based on this premise (to which I can hardly take
exception) the Parti Québécois' much heralded White
Paper is a massive document which tries to do for
Québec culture even more than the Massey Report intended in its time for Canadian culture in general. What
is novel in the Canadian context is, firstly, its extension
of the meaning of culture beyond the limited field of

160

education and the arts – even beyond the area of immigration to which Laporte had already extended it – to
take in almost every aspect of the society, and secondly,
the method of handling the document itself chosen by
the Québec Government.

On June 6, following several calculated leaks of
the draft document to selected members of the media the
previous week, the two-volume document was officially
made public.[5] The original work of its authors had been
cleansed and carefully watered down by politicians, so
much so that there are passages and recommendations
such as those relating to communications that are less
extreme than some of the proposals of Laurin's Liberal
predecessors. It is the product of the academic, or more
precisely, the sociologists' mind, massaged and moulded
by political interests. It is neither the product of what it
often refers to as indigenous Québec culture nor of an
attempt to understand what the majority of Québécois
wish, need or expect in the way of cultural policies,
activities or bureaucracies. As a consequence, the integrity of the volumes' thesis and proposals suffers. While the
message, often lyrical, is that only a sovereign Québec
can protect its culture, most of the proposals to be undertaken and financed in the immediate future can just as
easily be realized within the present constitutional framework. Though the authors have drawn upon the ideas of
the whole world (including Canada) for their conception
and suggestions, it is clear from a comparison of the final
version with earlier ones that what was once envisioned
as a scheme as sociologically comprehensive as that of
Sweden now proposes bureaucracies and institutions on a
scale that hardly matches those of France. Nonetheless, it
strikes me as an able and imaginative document which
puts culture, as I have tried to do in this essay, in its
central place. Only the means by which its main objectives are to be achieved are in controversy. It seems

doubtful that Québec could possibly finance all of them on its own, and there is little recognition of the reality that Québec has *not* been treated as a tributary of Ottawa and that the foundation of most of what the White Paper's recommendations must build on were paid for by Canadians as a whole. Here, as in so many other areas, Québec needs Canada. The document itself, in its grasp of the times we live in, should be proof in turn that Canada needs Québec.

One can only applaud the document's recognition of the integrative function of culture and admire the authors' skill in employing every powerful symbol and myth to enhance their case. But new institutions on the scale proposed will be immensely costly in terms of money and manpower. When one remembers that it took five years to implement just one of the Massey Commission's proposals (the establishment of the Canada Council), and then only after a windfall of succession duties, one cannot be optimistic about the early implementation of Dumont's pared-down proposals, even with the public support of so active and accomplished a politician as Laurin. They will face the same political obstacles as earlier proposals of the same kind. Indeed, the Parti Québécois' White Paper is rather like the delta at the mouth of the Nile: a rich sediment accumulated after many generations. It has great potential for growth. But will it prove fertile as Egypt's or barren like its Québec predecessors?

Dumont, Rioux and Laurin, Frégault, Laporte, Hardy, Tremblay and L'Allier all represent a particular and consistent stream of thought in Québec about the centrality of culture in the lives of Québécois which can only be achieved by a determined leadership and authoritarian governmental mechanisms. The only issue separating their proposals, which so often parallel Canadian federal or foreign institutions and programs, is whether

162

they should be conducted by a separate country and with a *dirigiste* style. But part of the tradition of all the white and green papers going back fifteen years, and indeed part of the reality of the rhetoric going back to Canon Groulx and Henri Bourassa, is that Québec governments have consistently shied away from acting seriously on such cultural proposals when their cabinets had to face up to the real costs. Is there reason to believe that this time it will be different?

While the new independantist government is organizing and building structures to carry forward its stated goals, carrying out studies and issuing statements and reports in order to refine a cultural policy of service to its followers and supporters. Québec artists are continuing their social involvement in the daily lives of their community as they have always done. Félix Leclerc has returned to the Ile d'Orléans and Vigneault sings about the Québécois as "people who love the sound of the spoken word." In the theatres, Dubé, Loranger, Tremblay and others express the problems, frustrations and joys of Québécois. The distinctiveness of Québec's musicians, poets and writers makes them well known outside the Province. The names of Québec's film-makers, painters, sculptors and other artists are respected throughout this continent and in several European countries. For some time those referred to as being part of "La Relève" have kept the chain unbroken. These artists have always been the popular conscience of Québécois. So that it would be a mistake to see in these activities since November 15, 1976, the destruction of the pro-Québec-in-Canada cultural argument in the province.

In a "political testament" submitted to *Le Devoir* on January 6, 1978, one of the province's cultural savants, Mgr. Félix-Antoine Savard, gave his view of the social and political situation in Québec today. After discussing language, education, the economy and the problems now

163

facing Québec, Mgr. Savard made the following comment:

> This is why, despite my respect for the separatist leaders, I am opposed to a doctrine which I believe is contrary to the order of things. . . . This is why I feel hostility toward this type of separatism which I believe runs counter to the vital interests of Québec, which would deprive it of the complementarity of culture, economy and language and of harmonious relationships with all Canadians, regardless of race or origin, that it needs in order to prosper.

Mgr. Savard's statement brought numerous and heated reactions. It provoked consternation among independentists who had identified themselves with the thoughts and work of the author of *Menaud maître-draveur*. The Cultural Minister Louis O'Neill was quick to return Mgr. Savard's fire: "You should read *Menaud* again. I am sure that doing so would help you to become reconciled with this new era which you view with such pessimism. Then you might feel like writing a completely different type of testament which would gladden the hearts of the thousands of Québécois who esteem and admire you" (*Le Devoir*, January 10, 1978).

And so the Great Debate that has troubled Québec for hundreds of years and Canadians since the mid-nineteenth century continues. Impassioned reactions followed Savard's intervention in the debate, among them that of Pierre Perrault, the author of more than ten films, including *Le Règne du Jour* and *Les Voitures d'eau*. A writer, poet and film-maker, Perrault had always regarded himself as a disciple of Savard. He expressed disappointment at the "testament": "This morning, once again, with no marquis intervening, I have been disinherited by my father." At the same time Yves Préfontaine, writing in the February 1977 issue of the *Canadian Arts Conference Bulletin*, reminded us that "In Québec, as elsewhere but more so, perhaps because of its special historical circumstances, the artists and creative people were and still are *the sound box* which sets the tone for what is certainly the deep anguish but also the great wealth of our snowbound little band of people."

Québec's artists were never divorced from those responsible for setting the stage for the vast social changes that occurred in their province in the sixties and seventies. The artistic community does not change with each election; it remains as real and as much a part of the people as life itself. A generation ago Duplessis was still trying to make Québec culture subservient to his politics. He lost that battle. But the war continues. It is now again the artists who are keeping a vigil to ensure that their peoples are not fooled. In the words of Vigneault, "I still have to build a place to stand."

The foregoing brief surveys in chapters five and six of federal and provincial approaches to the support of culture, however defined, should give some idea of the enormous surge of energy, billions of dollars and tens of thousands of bureaucrats being made available by both levels of government, and by professional and voluntary organizations in the private sector. And no mention has been made of municipal activities in this field, where in a city like Toronto there is already a budget of over $4 million reserved for cultural development.[6] It may be useful, if only to dispel the common anthropomorphic view of governments as unitary entities searching their pockets for dimes and nickels in miserly fashion, to give a brief account of how the new cultural bureaucracy generally functions at the federal level and in most provinces.

Grants to individuals tend to be left to the arts councils, where they exist. In dealing with applications for personal grants, the Canada Council has resorted to outside assessors, often meeting in juries, chosen from among the best available professionals in the disciplines or activities concerned, and these rosters are frequently changed. This seems to be the fairest way to proceed, but there is a danger, increasingly a subject of criticism, of inbreeding; an assessor is likely to favour an applicant whose skills or techniques or ideas resemble his own, thus creating a succession of potential assessors who are likely to perpetuate a particular school of thought.

In supporting arts organizations, the Canada Council is saddled with the obligation to provide sustaining grants, on a rapidly increasing scale, to the great "national" performing arts organizations, and is consequently left with proportionately decreasing funds for the support of promising new organizations. One solution recently suggested would be a program of cost-indexed sustaining grants to these organizations of national importance directly from the Department of the Secretary of State, leaving the Council to provide them with funds for new productions and special projects. The difficulty of obtaining a consensus on those that are of national importance might be overcome, as it has been in the museums field, but the nature of a museum is more permanent than that of a performing arts organization, which may go into a period of unacceptably declining professional standards to the point where it can no longer be regarded as of national importance. The Council is better placed to make such a judgment, as it does with theatre organizations, than a department or its minister.

The expenditures of departments on cultural activities and support are not decided in individual cases, as is commonly supposed, by individual bureaucrats. First, the programs must be fitted into overall departmental budg-

166

ets approved by a treasury board; very large special items have to go to Cabinet. The federal Treasury Board, for example, may, on the advice of its non-specialist staff, alter the internal balance of departmental programs, sometimes with unfortunate or even sadly comical results. A few years ago, for instance, it was decided to allow an inflationary percentage increase for the performing arts but not for the visual arts, in bland disregard for the fact that the cost of living had also gone up not only for artists but for the administrators of museums. Although the Canada Council is, legally speaking, free to spend its money as it pleases, it is dependent on allocations from current public funds, with the results that its internal balance between programs is also susceptible to a form of manipulation by the second guessors at Treasury Board and Secretary of State.

There is also a political angle to grants made by the federal government as such. In cutting up what may be called the cultural cake, priorities for the size and distribution of the slices have to be determined in two dimensions. One set of priorities relates to the apppropriate slices for each field of activity – the visual arts, the performing arts, ethnic and multicultural organizations, and the many disciplines covered by the humanities. A second set of priorities – and this is where political considerations necessarily come in – is aimed at achieving a reasonably equitable and, if possible, politically advantageous distribution of available resources among the provinces, regions and large cities. Thus, combining the two sets of priorities, it may be necessary to balance a theatre here against a museum there, a science centre in one place against the renovation of a historical landmark elsewhere, and so on.

Provincial governments face the same problems, within a more manageable area, in determining local priorities. If the personal knowledge of applicants and regular direct contacts with them plays an important part in making priority decisions, in some cases, regrettably, those decisions are too heavily influenced by the political orientation of the applicant, whether an organization or an individual. Applicants are thus aware that decisions are being taken by recognizable people, whereas federal decisions all too often have the appearance of being made by faceless bureaucrats. It is also true that the chances of receiving a federal grant may be governed to some extent by the tastes or prejudices of individual federal officials, but these are mostly countered by the collegial nature of recommendations to the minister and the Treasury Board. All of this "balancing" leaves the major question of quality and excellence rather further down the list of priorities in decision-making than it ought to be.

Many arts organizations and, in particular, individual artists have an uncomfortable feeling that it is somehow demeaning to have to go, cap in hand so to speak, asking for government handouts. Moreover, they are generally so absorbed in their own enthusiasms and needs as to be unable to perceive, even dimly, their place in the broader framework in which priorities must be set; all they can understand is that some bureaucrat has refused to give them what they regard as the absolute minimum for their operations, even for their continued existence. They do not hesitate to express themselves in these terms, and the word gets around that Canadian governments are not being as generous as they should be in support of culture. Unfortunately, there seems to be no way of avoiding the cap-in-hand process.

In fact, Canadian governments are pouring out money for culture, in all senses of the word, on a scale that would have been inconceivable even as recently as ten years ago and that is surpassed, relatively speaking, by few other countries in the world. Nevertheless, the institutions supported and the budgets provided just happen to have emerged, without anything like a conscious plan (except in Québec), without full awareness of the vital place of human imagination in the nation's life. This was evident as soon as the chill winds of recession began to blow across the world and the need for restraints on government spending became obvious. But by the time the federal government had come to examine its fiscal arrangements for 1978-79, cultural budgets had already been frozen and then cut following two or three fiscal years of financial increases which barely met costs due to inflation. The habit of timidity in the cultural area, despite all that had been learned over the years – and especially what ought to have been learned from Expo 67, from Canada Day 77 or from the cultural evolution of Québec in the past decade – had triumphed again.

And if we cannot learn from our own experience and reality, perhaps the federal government of Canada and its advisers would take a careful look at the recent experience and decisions on cultural policy of democracies that have always been friends and allies: Britain, France, Switzerland, Sweden and the United States.[7] Each of these countries, with the exception of Switzerland, has economic problems at least as severe as our own; each has at least as long and certainly as rich a cultural life and greater cultural resources relatively and absolutely; each has fewer political problems of national unity than we do while each has a form of government that permits easier administrative solutions. None, therefore, has as great a need to respond to the cultural needs expressed by its artists and population as does Canada. Yet in the past few years, each of these countries has undertaken or announced its intention to undertake policies and programs of public support for culture on a scale greater than at any comparable period in its history. That story is even more strikingly illustrated in several underdeveloped and socialist countries.

169

Underlying our Canadian timidity, I think, is the belief that culture is the flowering of affluence, a happy luxury, and as such, something to be cast aside in hard times. Another damaging belief is that the arts belong to snobs and rich people. I do not think it is possible to overstate the lesson dramatically brought home to us by Expo 67, that, like the Tivoli Gardens in Copenhagen or Ontario Place in Toronto, or the Discovery Train, the finest expressions of human imagination and art and skill belong to everyone. They are symbols of continuity, of community and renewal. What is more, it is precisely in hard times that the consolation of the arts is most needed. I am not thinking about escapist art either, though there is a place for that too. It is in hard times that the majority of Canadians ask themselves what they are doing here in these cold latitudes. Now more than ever men and women need the culture that confronts them with something beyond their own experience, the vision of reality which makes a common life possible. As Albert Einstein very simply put it: "Imagination is more important than knowledge."

But perhaps there is more than timidity in the air. At the very moment when the federal and provincial institutions concerned with cultural matters are beginning to make something like a coherent pattern, and an organization has grown up which needs only the animating spirit of a conscious policy to make it effective, there are signs of failing confidence, of political neglect. Instead of following up the inspiration of Expo '67, it looks as if we are developing a future that will succeed only in achieving the bureaucratization of culture. Something that can only be called sourness has begun to poison the springs of action.

The growth of national disillusion and decline of political support for culture outside of Québec but particularly in Ottawa can be glimpsed in many directions.

There have been attacks on the Canada Council by its clients as well as by politicians. The unity of vision which placed assistance to the social sciences and humanities under the same roof with assistance to the arts has been replaced by a view that splitting the Council is somehow now more effective.[8] There have been attacks on the CBC by freelance artists put out of work by budget cuts, on the CRTC by clients angered at its surrender to the new technology and to Americanization, and on both by politicians who feel they have been given, so to say, a bad press. Attempts at co-operation between federal and provincial cultural institutions too often fail. Above all, the preoccupation of politicians and to some extent of the press with the faltering economy and the threats to national unity has led to neglect of culture. The centrality of cultural policy to the success of both the economy and the polity has been forgotten once again.

In the resulting atmosphere of discouragement and cynicism, the increasingly centralized administration of arts patronage has merely achieved an opportunity and a temptation to subject arts institutions to political manipulation. Though the great danger is that of cultural direction, another danger exists which is often overlooked – that politicians will interfere with the decisions of professionals for no better reason than to express their own personal tastes. As Lord Goodman, when chairman of the British Arts Council, was fond of saying to people responsible for patronizing the arts, "You should never be afraid of your own opinion – you should be terrified of it."

The existence of these dangers is yet another argument for a comprehensive federal-provincial policy on culture, openly arrived at. Without it, cultural institutions are at the mercy of capricious adventurers and political expediency.

In the face of such discouraging possibilities, it

171

may seem foolishly optimistic to say that the outlook is far from hopeless, that we could be on the brink of great achievements. The fact is that there is a good and a bad aspect to all our mental habits. Our habit of toleration can also be a habit of neglect; our habit of regional patriotism can also be one of provincial isolation; our habit of cultural freedom one of cultural Babel. In the sour mood of the late seventies, it is possible to believe the worst about ourselves. But perhaps it would be more sensible to persist in believing the best.

The cultural institutions which we have created in this country are among the finest and most sophisticated in the modern world. Canadians have proved beyond doubt their creative capacity in all the arts and sciences as well as in the application of imagination to commerce.

It is disquieting to find that, with all this going for us, there is a temptation to return to bickering and the law of the jungle.

Canada ... is better off as she stands than she would be as a member of a confederacy composed of five sovereign states, which would be the result if the powers of the local governments were not defined. A strong central government is indispensable to the success of the experiment we are trying.

Sir John A. Macdonald, 1864.

Je me souviens.

Eugène Taché, 1883.

Nationhood is a common goal, a continual creation of our joint efforts. ... To be together is an enormous undertaking, an infinitely complex orchestration of which the invisible leader is the shared conviction that this sense of togetherness exists, that it has meaning through history, that we must be careful that we don't let it slip away and that this concern at several levels is synonymous with freedom, democracy, social justice and humanity. The gravest disaster that can threaten a people is not military annihilation; it is the indifference of its members to the shape of their future.

Pierre Emmanuel, 1971.

We have been the first – and in many ways the only – people to be affected in a deep and lasting fashion by the three major currents of contemporary thought and genius: the English, the French and the American. ... But now we have the strength, the numbers and the self-confidence to choose what suits us, to assimilate it and give it originality, thus creating a civilization of many cultures – the only kind that can survive. ...

H. E. Governor General
Jules Léger, 1974.

A culture thrives where there is a centre ... that vivifies the efforts of those involved. ... The fragmentation of culture into compartmentalized segments inevitably tend(s) to break up the discourse which sustains a culture for the entire society.

Daniel Bell, 1976.

SEVEN

It should be clear by now that Canadian governments have committed large resources to the support of culture, whether we define it in the narrower sense of the arts or in the wider sense that includes language, education, communications or recreation. The federal, provincial and municipal bureaucracies that administer support to culture are formidable; the culture industry itself is an employer to be reckoned with in all parts of the country. The institutions that have been developed to share cultural resources, such as the network of associate museums and exhibition centres aided by grants from the National Museums, may be unique in the world. The administration of culture has become a big beautiful machine. Only the mind in the machine is missing.

The machine will not be able to achieve much without a clear and new recognition by government and public alike of the special need in Canada for a comprehensive policy of cultural development. And this need has always been with us; responding to it constructively now should be done with a clear perspective of our entire

175

history avoiding if possible an exaggerated reaction to any single event such as occurred on November 15, 1976.

I have argued that cultural development should be a central goal of governments because it means giving a society the ability to create its own life and environment; and that it is also the process by which that goal is achieved. In this argument I am at one both with my intellectual enemies in the camps of the separatist or totalitarian ideologies in Québec and the communist world, and with my cultural allies in the liberal and social democracies of western Europe. Only in the North American democratic environment is this definition still largely unacceptable to the cultural priesthood and its political leaders. But I am convinced the Canadian attitude will change. It will or there will not be a Canada. The need to create our own life and environment becomes more and more urgent as we feel the pressures to conform to the largely unconscious Americanization which acts on us through technology, advertising and other engines of commercial persuasion, as well as through the popular arts. The dramatic speed with which the technological overflow of telecommunications multinationals moves does not even allow us the freedom to pace our own lives. Even such distinctive institutions as our courts of law are seen through eyes educated by United States television. That state of affairs cannot be allowed to continue indefinitely: even some provincial governments, impatient with federal inaction, have moved to try to stem the tide in certain areas.

The pressures of modernizing Americanization are toward uniformity, homogeneity and conformity. A policy of cultural development would seek to promote diversity and pluralism, correcting the tendencies inherent in mass marketing and mass entertainment to limit cultural choices. It follows that government support to the arts, in the interest of pluralism, is nearly always support to the

176

preferences of minorities. Money, in other words, is taken from all the taxpayers and spent on a few of them. There is a false populism which rejects this principle as undemocratic, though in fact the whole fiscal policy of Canadian Confederation works the same way.

But perhaps a federal cultural policy has to do more than provide support to minority culture of all kinds – provincial, regional, ethnic, or simply esoteric. Individual choice, and even individual caprice, should be jealously protected, but the cultural development of the whole nation, with all its diversity, will entail a conscious effort to discover and cultivate "the things we cherish" in common, a quest for that consensus that Jacques Rigaud has called "the single spiritual and moral breath of an entire community."

The problem will be to discover such a consensus and such a community in Canada, a country whose identities are legion and scattered over a vast geographical area. Although it is probably true that all nation states are more or less pluralistic and subject to centrifugal strains, Canada may be unique in its apparent incoherence. Most unitary states have been helped in the quest for community by the bonds created by external wars and dangers or by educational systems that teach a common history or common myths, creating understanding, perspective and a sense of belonging. In democracies, the party system often has the same effect. But Canadian federal parties seem to have had the opposite result, frequently assisting provincial counterparts whose policies, by a Canadian paradox, have been anti-federal. Relations between federal and provincial governments, whose politicians are elected by the same voters, have sometimes been conducted as though they were foreign to each other. The resulting conflicts have been potent sources of those divisive myths I noted earlier.

A sense of the nation, which neither schools nor

political parties seem capable of promoting, can be discovered through common cultural experience. Where the experience has not been "common," it can still be shared. A federal policy can provide the links, the connections or the opportunities for sharing and connecting. A continuing quest for a comprehensive national policy on culture, including a canvass of the whole country, would itself help to create this experience. In a real sense such a quest would by its nature help to build connections. No matter how tight a regional sense of community may be, no matter how committed to secession a region or province may feel, it is the function of the central government in a genuine federation to try to build connections and link these communities, provinces and regions into a larger whole, to try through imagination to reach out and convince them to see and to sense the larger community, Canada. If it ceases consciously to try, and if it should eventually fail, it ceases to serve the chief purpose for which it was originally created. And the confederation ceases to exist.

We also have to live with the facts of our nature. Canada will remain a confederation with two official languages and many local and increasingly regionally distinct cultures, and at least one of these European-American cultures will always seek and obtain a special place in the Canadian environment. We shall remain a people whose educational and political processes are fragmented. And we shall always be neighbour to the much more powerful and uniform United States in an era when there are no such things as cultural frontiers. "Life laughs at cultural locksmiths," as Morley Callaghan argued in a recent essay.[1] Cultural policy cannot lock out American influence; it can only seek to strengthen Canadian self-confidence. So that when I referred a moment ago to discovering a consensus, as in most political matters Canadian, the word tends to mean something a little

178

different than it might in other countries. The most we can probably hope for is agreement on *some* of the objectives of cultural development in Canada, not a uniform cultural policy: cultural co-existence for traditional British and French cultures and, as George Ignatieff has stated, "a sort of Maoist 'let many flowers bloom' for the rest." The process of achieving these objectives should contribute to a better and deeper understanding and tolerance of our multiculturalism and should spring from a deeper or heightened awareness of the origins of Canadian culture.

Of course, there is a danger that politicians, once aroused to a sense of the importance of culture, will see it as a tool of policy, the way it is seen and used in socialist and fascist republics and as it is used on occasion in one or two Canadian provinces already. This danger seems more immediate in the present decade than it might have been in the past, as there has been a trend to the politicization of writers and artists. Not only have writers and artists themselves become more "engaged" in the seventies, but a number of politically motivated intellectuals have taken up culture as a ladder to power and influence or used political influence as an entrée to the world of culture. It has been a decade of skilful lobbying by the arts community, especially in obtaining increased amounts of federal money. Vigilance will be needed to ensure that artists and writers are not seduced by political pressures. As one of my political philosophy teachers at London University, the late R. H. Tawney, was fond of repeating to his students, "Political ambitions make good servants but bad masters."

At this stage, there is little need to call for greatly increased federal involvement in the support of culture, still less for greatly increased federal spending. But one must repeat, "at this stage." Without knowing a good deal more than we do at present, we cannot be certain that there is already enough public funding in aid of culture. We do know there is not enough private funding; not enough entrepreneurial capacity in seeking out private donors, and not enough incentive for the private sector to respond to. Without a conscious policy there is no way of knowing how much is enough and how much too much. There is evidence of a disproportion between expenditures on facilities and on content and not only in broadcasting. A leading Canadian theatre personality thinks there may now be more jobs, of all kinds, in Canadian theatre than there are competent Canadians to fill them. There is evidence of a disproportion between expenditures on facilities in the nation's capital and facilities in provincial capitals, and on facilities in some regions when compared with the real needs of others. There is a danger that more money will be spent on the cultural bureaucracies and cultural middlemen than on the culture itself or on the sharing and connecting of the cultures. Which is not to deny the necessity for bureaucrats and middlemen, the art clergy as it were, but only to say that what justifies them is the extent to which they help artists and writers to do their work and share it with fellow citizens.

For I persist in believing that what keeps any culture alive is the free activity of human imagination, expressed in significant form. Though art and science are in a sense international, reaching beyond their own place and time, the idea and image of a nation resides in the best that has been thought and felt and imagined by its artists and writers, its scientists and historians. The territory itself, which makes so strong a claim on the hearts of Canadians, is not perceived until it has been transformed into symbols by artists. There is a Jewish joke about the mother whose daughter was praised for her beauty. "But wait till you see her photograph," the mother said. Like most jokes, this one embodies a truth, that beauty often

180

does not exist for the beholder until it has been reflected in art.

The first concern of cultural policy will be with the liberation of creative imagination wherever it is found, with support to those with the gifts to take advantage of it for their art. A second concern will be with conservation of the Canadian heritage and environment. The Canadian heritage should be understood to include everything Canadians cherish, no matter from what source: it includes Beethoven as well as Claude Champagne, Mark Twain as well as Stephen Leacock, Rembrandt as well as Iskowitz, the whooping crane as well as the harp seal, the Ursuline Convent in Québec City as well as the Powder Magazine at Fort Anne. Our age is eclectic and, what is more, indigenous art has never flourished in isolation. The great surges of the Western imagination have always followed the discovery or rediscovery of earlier art; at the Renaissance, the rediscovery of the art of Greece and Rome; at the Romantic revolution, the rediscovery of the Middle Ages. English poetry began, one might say, when Geoffrey Chaucer translated Boccaccio's *Il Filostrato* into his native tongue. A policy of cultural development does not close doors, it opens them.

There are two other obvious lines of development: the first in education, training and competition of artists and craftsmen, the assurance of excellence; and the second in promoting culture and making it accessible in all parts of the country so that Canadians will come to know the different environments as well as the cultural backgrounds of the peoples who inhabit all the pieces of this sprawling land.

A start might be made toward policy development in all these directions, and indeed it has been made by some of the various mechanisms within the federal and provincial agencies involved. What is needed is more co-ordination and sharing of resources. The federal government might begin in its own backyard, so to speak, by acting upon the results of meetings between federal departments of government that daily have a major impact on our cultural life: the central agencies of the Treasury Board and the Privy Council Office, and the departments such as Finance, Urban Affairs, Communications, Public Works, Regional Economic Expansion, Transport, Environment, Health and Welfare, Industry, Trade and Commerce, the Post Office, National Defence, Indian and Northern Affairs and of course the Secretary of State. Only the last two or three departments have made a special point of considering the cultural aspect of their policies. But all these federal entities could concentrate on ways of sharing and exchanging information and ideas, seeking co-operation between representatives of the provinces, of the national cultures, within English-speaking Canada, between English and French Canada, and between both of these and the other cultures. They do not co-operate or co-ordinate their activities in the cultural field today because they are entirely unconscious of the fact that what they do often has cultural implications not only for the technical or social goals of their respective departments or specific clients but also for Canadian society as a whole.

Anyone who has first-hand experience of the way big bureaucracies work will be skeptical about the chances of getting government agencies to work together in this way. In prosperous times they have been accustomed to fight each other for their share of the available resources. In hard times, the country cannot afford this kind of arm-wrestling. Only a comprehensive policy discussed publicly and aired fully, including through the Cabinet and parliamentary process and through federal-provincial meetings, can assure a sensible division of resources and responsibilities. Indeed, the Privy Council

Office could take a lead immediately by insisting that all federal policy memoranda prepared for Cabinet discussion contain a section on cultural implications. Provincial cabinets might follow such a lead.

Within the federal bureaucracy, the officers of the Department of the Secretary of State and the senior members of federal cultural agencies have a special role. There can no longer be any excuse for delaying discussions and decisions on the underlying principles that must govern the conduct of these agencies: to identify their clients; to establish clearer distinctions between potential and excellence in their grant programs; to differentiate between equity and equality in interpreting and applying pluralism to their procedures; to clarify the criteria that must govern their relations with artists, professional organizations and provinces alike; and to wrap up the first stage of the debate on their internal managerial affairs so that there are assurances that the pieces are all contributing to the whole on publicly understood and acceptable definitions and priorities.

But it is not the purpose of this essay to offer an academic study of the problems or to draft a federal Cabinet document outlining what a comprehensive policy might be that would prove acceptable to the framers of the new Canadian constitution. Cultural policy, since it touches on the values and beliefs of all Canadians, cannot be developed secretly inside the walls of government offices and then imposed on the people. Such a policy would either be harmful or completely ineffective. If harmful it would certainly be resisted, if not, it would die of inanition. The process of arriving at the policy is as important as the policy itself. There should be a strenuous effort to include as many Canadians as possible if the national consciousness is to be raised to the point where cultural issues – normally unconscious – are perceived as vitally important. Only a deliberate canvass of

183

the country's interested citizens, institutions, federal, provincial and municipal bureaucrats and politicians, artists, critics, publicists, scholars in the sciences and arts, craftsmen of every sort, writers and musicians, representatives of the passive consumers of cultural products, broadcasters and others can generate the popular support to implement their policies and programs. Success in this area might point the way for others.

The first and most pressing need is for information, for hard statistical facts. Statistical studies, it is true, are slow to develop, but they are still necessary. Useful data have been produced from time to time by several museums, the Canada Council and the Ontario Theatre group, for example. Statistics Canada, through the Survey of Cultural Institutions and the Survey of Selected Leisure Activities (1972 and 1975), conducted on behalf of the Secretary of State, is beginning to develop a cultural-indicator database system.[2] The Department of Recreation at the University of Waterloo has developed a leisure studies databank. The Department of Fine Arts at York University, Toronto, for several years has been developing a comprehensive bibliography on Canadian cultural subject matter. What is lacking is a continuing commitment to the research capacity by these institutions and the encouragement of the public interest to interpret and develop multiple-analysis formats for use in policy development.

It is more than a decade since Alvin Toffler wrote "The Art of Measuring the Arts," calling for a cultural data system "to provide information for national policy-making in the cultural field and to assist those outside the field in understanding their impact on it."[3] No progress has yet been made in the United States or elsewhere on the tentative model he constructed in 1967, although in the past few months the demand from the U.S. Congress for accurate information and analyses of arts ex-

184

penditures has forced the National Endowment for the Arts to undertake a massive new research program. Canada, with modest resources, could achieve a sophisticated national cultural indicators' program today if the existing data-collecting system were expanded and modified and a capability developed for using the information in policy studies. To put it another way, we already have some of the raw material for a sound information base. We need more on a guaranteed continuity basis; but above all, we need the capacity to analyse it and build from there. Canadian government departments and agencies in co-operation with our universities and public and private research institutions, have the capacity and should get on with it. And having done that, they should find the means to explain their conclusions in terms that make sense to artists, politicians, bureaucrats and the electorate.

We have already observed that such information as we do possess has not become general knowledge. More surprising perhaps, it has not made a noticeable impression on Canadian politicians. We have seen how the findings of certain surveys showed that grants given to the performing arts had resulted in a profit to the treasury, in addition to the employment and enjoyment they had given. It is just this sort of information that needs to be made known to larger audiences. And also to smaller ones. No social scientist to my knowledge has taken up the call of John Meisel to examine more closely the relationship between politics and culture, nor have Canadian political scientists heeded the criticism of one of their profession when, in 1970, Bruce Doern stated that "it is safe to say that part of the reason why the officials within government, at both the political and bureaucratic levels, have had difficulties in beginning to conceptualize the policy-making structures of the 1970s is because Canadian political scientists have offered very

185

little to support this most difficult enterprise."[4] There would be far less need for concern about Americanization (or Anglicization) if more Canadian scholars would get on with the challenges of their chosen professions at the time these appear.

Information is also badly needed about the costs of cultural development and the alternative sources available for meeting such costs. How much needs to be spent on buildings, theatres and other facilities; how much on education and training; how much on conservation; how much on direct support to artists and writers; how much on ensuring excellence; how much on analyses of and dissemination of information about the information collected and on the broad promotion of our achievements? There should be surveys of the sources of financing such investigations, whether from federal, provincial, municipal, private foundation, business or labour sources, of the extent to which the burdens are shared, and in what proportions. Above all, there should be some effort to discover where, within these sources, assistance has never been forthcoming but might be, and the probable limits of financing from all these sources. All these surveys, analyses and data-collecting might be anathema to the creative mind but they are essential ingredients for governmental decision-making, not make-work programs for social scientists.

The relationship between our tax system and our need for greater art collections of quality is one more kind of example of the type of information to be aired publicly:[5] the future of Loto Canada's increasing revenues is another.[6] The effort alone might do something to halt the present tendency to see new public spending (and therefore collecting) on culture as the solution to all cultural ills. It is significant that when the budgets of some cultural institutions are cut, such as the CBC, the resulting economies are almost invariably and perhaps

186

unavoidably made in programming, not in administration or capital projects, which are not amenable to violent short-term fluctuations.

Finally, a great deal more needs to be known about the culture industry as a whole, how effective its distribution system is, what the economic position of most artists is, how far the industry contributes toward full employment or tourism or mental health; how far it is perceived to contribute to a sense of identity and community. At present few departments of government, federal or provincial, show any interest in these questions. University departments, funded largely by the same taxpayers, show even less interest.

If all this sounds humdrum and bureaucratic, it is because there is a lot of tough questioning to be done before we can begin to see where we are and where we might be going in cultural development. And also because we are talking about government and this is the nature of the beast. There is a prosy aspect to all government doings. The facts must be collected that deal with the basic informational needs of those who wish to join in the policy debate. These facts must be analysed in language and in a manner that lends itself to a practical debate of complex issues by the broad public. And the analyses must have a wide distribution to both of the official language groups of this country; a fact that Messrs. Laurin and Dumont might usefully consider.

The "management of discontent" takes time. While the necessary information is being gathered and analysed, there are a number of issues to be discussed and debated. The role – real, perceived or needed – of the federal, provincial and municipal governments in cultural development is one of them. As John Porter noted in *The Vertical Mosaic*, the theory of Canadian federalism is that each province constitutes a particular variety of culture which federalism must safeguard.[7] The role of the federal government in culture is really not unlike its role in other segments of society and the market economy. The foundation of a democratic society is the individual human person, possessing inalienable rights which rise above capital, tradition, the church or the state. Federalism is a system of counterweights. Government is the only institution that can respond to the powerful and the privileged, to the impact of large multinational corporations and trade unions; it is supposed to intervene or make regulations to protect the individual against combinations, restrictive practices and cartels. In the liberal democratic philosophy that has dominated Canadian political life it is supposed to free the market economy, safeguard individual choice and assist the humble and the meek.

In cultural matters, where freedom of choice is threatened by the sheer volume of mass persuasion and mass culture and by the uniformity that results from competition for mass markets, it is probably only the federal government that has the power and resources to intervene and ensure the survival on a national scale of alternative cultural products. Only the federal government has the interest and responsibility to ensure the broad dissemination of information about the alternative choices available. Canadians, to put it another way, need to be free to choose Canadian culture, and they cannot be free in this way if the culture they prefer has been bulldozed or fragmented out of existence. Therefore, some protection of the Canadian producer and distributer of whatever region or province is inevitable. Which is not to deny for a moment the right of any citizen to choose a McDonald hamburger if that is what he wants. It is merely to say that if he happens to prefer a falafel or a tourtière he should be able to buy that too. To buy it, he has to know of its existence first, to have some familiarity with its value or worth. He or she must then know how to buy it, and, finally have the means not only to buy it but also to judge whether it turned out to be a good buy. So that it will be greatly to the consumer's advantage if there is more than one outlet.

A policy of cultural development will always have these goals of liberty and choice in view. It cannot take the form of a plan for dictating the course of development of the arts. The motions of imagination are unpredictable, even disconcerting. It is a well-known attribute of imaginative work that it is not always responsive to routine and planning. Even in the sciences, discoveries are made (I am thinking of the great discoveries) by minds which are playing hooky from their regular work. One thinks of Sir Alexander Fleming, who discovered penicillin when, almost daydreaming, he began to wonder about the accident which had caused a certain mould to grow on one of his slides, spoiling a carefully planned experiment. Or of James Watson who, in his book *The Double Helix*, cheerfully reports how he was obliged to lie to the foundation supporting him in order to pursue his real work, the search for the DNA molecule, which any responsible functionary would have considered outside his competence. He did not know enough mathematics for a start.

There is a whole body of testimony to this intractability of imaginative work to regulation. Some have compared the work of invention to fishing. Others say it is like night vision in which, in order to see something in the dark, one has to look away from it. And at least one successful Canadian novelist, John Buell, has never asked for a Canada Council grant because he is certain that the sense of duty it would entail would dry up his inspiration.

This may explain why there has been a tendency on the part of cultural agencies to turn in embarrassment from the producers of creative work and offer their

189

money instead to the middlemen and functionaries who earn their money as midwives to the arts. Or to favour organizations of artists rather than artists themselves. There are other reasons, as we have seen, why politicians and public functionaries feel uncomfortable with artists. "You are feeding the hand that bites you," Kildare Dobbs told the Liberal Thinkers study conference in Kingston in 1960. To recall Rigaud, culture is also the denial of collective certainties. No culture can survive without change and criticism; changes in sensibility are initiated by artists – and nearly always experienced as shocking. The idea of spending public money in order to be shocked and made uncomfortable is sure to be frightening. That is why it is important that the institutions through which the arts are supported are kept at arm's length from political influence and that there be more than one political door to go to for public funding as there is for private.

The principle is well understood in most democracies. Kenneth Robinson, a former Labour minister, now chairman of the Arts Council of Great Britain, defended the principle in the 1977 Alport Lecture in London. Speaking of the Council, he said:

> For the first time in Britain's history, and I believe in the history of any nation, a body existed, financed but not interfered with by government, for the purpose of sustaining, promoting, subsisting and distributing the arts in the widest sense of that term. It has been described as a typically British solution and in the best sense I firmly believe that to be true. As predecessors of mine have declared on more than one occasion, it is in every way a solution superior to that of a fully-fledged Ministry of the Arts, such as exists in some countries of Europe.

Why do I assert that an Arts Council is preferable to a Ministry of Culture? There are in my view a number of arguments, all pointing in the same direction. Public support for the arts and in particular the distribution of funds for this purpose, inevitably involve issues of taste, opinion and subjective judgment. Decisions have to be made over an enormous field, ranging from some large and important decisions directly affecting the cultural life of the nation, right through to a multiplicity of minor decisions mainly affecting individuals. Is it not better that ultimate responsibility for such decisions should lie with a group of individuals chosen for their interest in and knowledge of the arts generally – or one or two in particular – voluntarily giving their time and experience to the cause, than to a single individual who as a Minister cannot be immune from political pressures, and as a man from personal predilection and prejudice, and who on the law of averages would hold the job for less than two years? Furthermore is it not preferable that the decision-makers should be supported by officials and advisers who are chosen for their specialist knowledge and expertise and who themselves choose this role as a career, rather than by persons who, however intelligent and cultured, are essentially birds of passage moving sooner or later to some other government department?

The Arts Council is not unique in its relationship to central government. The Research Councils, medical, agricultural, social science, are comparable, as is the University Grants Committee. Government determines after due consultation with the body concerned the quantum, but distribution is firmly delegated to that body. If it is inconceivable that this pattern of independence from Government should not apply in research and in higher education, and I think it is, why should not the same principle apply in the perhaps even more difficult and controversial area of the arts?[8]

In Canada, the Massey Commission quoted an earlier chairman of the Arts Council of Great Britain, Lord Keynes, who said in 1945:

Everyone, I fancy, recognizes that the work of the artist in all its aspects is, of its nature, individual and free, undisciplined, unregimented and uncontrolled. The artist walks where the breath of the spirit blows him. He cannot be told his direction; he does not know it himself.... The task of an official body is not to teach or censor, but to give courage, confidence and opportunity.

In pursuit of this principle the Massey Commission frowned on the idea of annual votes of money to arts institutions, though they have since come to be the practice in all federal and provincial cultural bodies. At least one critic,[9] indeed, feared that the independence of the Canada Council was compromised when, in 1972, it accepted large subventions from the Secretary of State's Department specifically earmarked for aid to Canadian-owned publishing houses. Against that opinion is the statement of former Secretary of State Gérard Pelletier, who said in 1970, "In our view, there is no alternative to individual creative initiative and a government should not only respect the freedom of the artist and scholar, but also provide for the independence of public institutions so that the specialists who direct them may base their actions on professional rather than political criteria."[10] This stand has been reiterated by provincial ministers too, in particular Robert Welch of Ontario.[11] It goes without saying that politicians would be wise not to attempt professional artistic judgments, and perhaps it is time a federal prime minister once again made such a philosophy publicly his government's. To my knowledge, no Québec prime minister or minister of culture has ever supported publicly this "arm's-length" philosophy, though Claude Ryan has just recently stated that should he be elected to power in Québec he would immediately create a cultural council, modeled on the Canada Council, and *independent* of the administration of the Québec Department of Cultural Affairs. (*Le Devoir*, June 10, 1978).

The best defence against infringements of this principle, for whatever reason, is an informed and articulate public opinion. Here the role of the media, the press and the critics is important, but it is in the nature of their work that they seldom, if ever, initiate discussion of cultural issues. Holding the mirror up to the age, they are equipped to react and respond rather than to take a lead. The trade unions, too, are unfortunately similarly equipped. Let us hope that the recently established Association of Cultural Executives will do better. But in the final analysis, what protection is there from either a President of the Treasury Board who finds the purchase of Renaissance paintings by the National Gallery neither to his taste nor to his politics, or from a fickle Secretary of State who might fancy he knows better than curators or directors, the relative value of objects to the collections, whether they be Carolingian ivories or military medals, other than the professional standards of bureaucrats, the vigilance of representative boards of citizens and, above all, an informed public?

I have suggested that cultural policy should not be developed inside government offices, even when responsible officials take the trouble to seek advice from influential persons in the arts community across the country. In the past, as we have seen, important cultural institutions in Canada have nearly always come into existence as the result of initiatives from voluntary organizations, from passionately interested individuals and societies or from massive royal commissions which involved large sections of the population. Not only was the CBC conceived in this way but also the Massey and B&B commissions, and though it was often a governor general who took up the cause of culture, he was always prompted by an interested individual, an artist or a group of artists. But to suggest that policy should not be developed entirely within government walls is not to say that government should either be ignorant of its role or merely responsive to client pressures. Government and Parliament have a responsibility to hold a view and take a stand. Federal institutions, as I have indicated earlier, must define for themselves what *they* mean by culture and on what principles they intend to conduct their affairs in the public or national interest. They must be able to show and defend the bureaucratic connection inside the machine. And they must parley with their colleagues in the provincial and voluntary sectors.

The initiative for a policy of cultural development, for a policy that would organize federal, provincial, municipal and private activities in culture into some sort of coherence, should come from the voluntary sector. A body or co-operating bodies similar to the Canadian Conference of the Arts – one democratically run, representative of many groups of artists and art professionals, genuinely pluralistic in terms of language and ethnicity in its structure, fairly reflective of the major regions – could begin to plan a series of national meetings across the country, open to all citizens, and sponsored and funded by federal, provincial, corporate and individual backers. Its aim would be to arouse public interest in cultural development and canvass opinion on what direction it should take. Such open meetings in the O'Keefe Centre in the sixties and similar ones dealing with related subjects held at the National Arts Centre and elsewhere in the seventies have attracted widespread attention in the media. At a point in our history when constitutional issues and culture are inevitably intertwined, the results of such forums are essential to future generations.

Meetings of this kind would involve everyone who cares about the arts and cultural matters and would attract the attention of others who have perhaps not hitherto given thought to their importance. They might also avoid the tired old jurisdictional disputes that tend to be brought on by royal commissions and task forces created and demanded by governments. They might even succeed in minimizing debate over the shortcomings of the press, CBC and "the feds" that have too long bored such assemblies during the few moments when some delegate is not bleating about an isolated silliness of the Canada Council. But to be really useful they would have to be on the one hand sufficiently structured to deal with the carefully organized and disseminated analytical and statistical material referred to earlier and, on the other hand, to be "open" enough to provide the flexibility that a mixed group appropriately challenged needs for its intellectual and emotional expression.

These are the most important reasons why a new Royal Commission on culture (as a follow-up on the Massey Commission) is probably not the way to go about developing cultural policy today. In 1973 I thought that it might be and made formal official recommendations to that effect. Later, I encouraged Hamilton Southam and certain voluntary agencies to press for one and they did. At about this time, Senator Lamontagne was trying to interest the Senate in a similar investigation but to no

195

avail. When it was obvious that a Royal Commission or Senate Committee was not in the cards, I recommended a task force reporting to the Secretary of State, supported by his department but with assistance coming also from other federal departments and institutions to study the question and report to the Cabinet within twelve months. Its chief purpose was to have been to inform ministers of some of the more outrageous anomalies within the federal system and indicate mechanisms and policies to put the federal culture house in order and make it more central to decision-making. Above all it was to define culture insofar as federal activities were concerned and enunciate the principles upon which this policy and future programming would be based, so that one could begin rational discussions with provincial counterparts. That too failed to materialize for reasons not entirely clear to me, considering the level of support the proposal had received. Finally I tried to persuade a group of Ottawa's most senior public servants to interest themselves more regularly and co-operatively in cultural issues and particularly in the problems of waste resulting from lack of federal co-ordination. But even such limited goals produced few concrete results. These experiences taught me that today, unlike 1949, the first problem in making policy for cultural development is to convince a larger number of responsible people to perceive its importance, no easy task when one remembers that culture itself tends to be unconscious – invisible, odourless and transparent as the air we breathe. The manner in which the recent Québec White Paper has been produced and manipulated for political purposes adds to my concern that the process be voluntary, public and widespread.

There may well be an honest school of thought which perceives the importance of culture but believes the best thing to do about it is to leave it alone. To do nothing is also a policy. Readers may recall that in the movie *Lawrence of Arabia*, when this possibility was suggested to General Allenby, in the person of the late Jack Hawkins, the general murmured, "It's usually best. . . ." There are times when masterly inaction is the wisest course. It may even be the most popular. When Alexander the Great offered his patronage to Diogenes the Cynic, asking what he could do for him, the philosopher said, "Stand out of my light!" Dr. Johnson is famous for the rudeness with which he rejected the patronage of Lord Chesterfield; it had come too late to help him.[12]

To return to the question whether a policy of inaction is reasonable in cultural development, the answer in this day and age has to be no. Without government subsidies the performing arts would falter and die, the symphony orchestras fall silent, the composers, writers and artists turn to other occupations. Even the richest and most free-market committed Americans have come around to this view. Without public subsidy there would be no libraries, museums, galleries or arts and science centres, and few Canadian books, films or broadcast programs. The quality of life in Canadian cities and towns would sink to an intolerable level; the power of Canadians to create their own life and environment would disappear.

And even if government subsidies and programs of support for the arts and sciences, for bilingualism and multiculturalism, were to continue indefinitely on their present basis, the absence of a comprehensive policy would allow bureaucracies and individual ministers to follow their own laws of growth unchecked. A simple illustration of this may be seen in provincial school systems where growing budgets are not matched by a reduction in the numbers of pupils in each classroom, and where the big rewards seem to go to those educators who are least in touch with the students.

A policy of development that involves all sectors

197

of the community might also put limits on bureaucratic growth.

(This lack of a comprehensive policy must not be viewed as merely a feature of the cultural scene; it is equally common of many areas of government activity. But it is beyond the scope of this essay to demonstrate how the habit of conducting administration by ad hoc responses to pressures swells the volume of government business without solving the problems. "Hunch, or guess-work..." was how the 1971 Report of the Economic Council of Canada[13] described governments' normal decision-making process.)

At this very moment a new threat arising from technological innovation demands immediate response, and at costs that could certainly be unprecedented, depending on whether Canadians perceive it as a threat or an opportunity. I am thinking not only of the implication of the "Information Society" which we have been warned about with increasing urgency for more than a decade, but also of the inevitable expanded use of the cable carrier for television.

The cultural implications of the imminent application of this technology for a country like ours – if we are to keep some semblance of individuality and independence – are alarming.[14] The problems are not with the electronic services for metre-reading, mail, cash and food delivery or safety devices. At the very least, Canadians will have to deal with the introduction of video-discs, video tape recorders, pay TV and home computers capable of storing and retrieving books, magazines and newspapers of every description. The problem in principle is similar to the one faced by Aird fifty years ago. How will Canadians want to use the cable (or fibre optic) which enters their homes, given the infinite choices it can offer of foreign products, culture, education?

There are a number of possible solutions to this

198

problem. For example, Canadians could simply allow the cable to develop the way it has been going for the last few years. This would mean letting the cable companies open the pay TV and home computer markets (electronic newspapers, magazines, books, and so on). Given the past performance of the industry, it seems unlikely that this would contribute to the growth of Canadian culture. It might give the cable companies an effective monopoly of all new services. Not only could this restrict diversity of information, it might also limit freedom of speech and technological innovation.

An alternative suggested by a number of commentators[15] is to change the status of cable. Instead of treating it in the traditional fashion, it could be considered as a common carrier – like the telephone companies – and regulated as a public utility. Among other things, this would give independent producers and programmers access to the electronic distribution system. It could open the way for repeat channels, special interest channels, regional and minority group channels, and even the kind of vertically programmed system recommended recently by Stuart Griffiths in his study for the Ontario Royal Commission on Violence in Broadcasting.[16] Some such arrangement would permit a new approach to the regulation of the range of cultural activity delivered electronically, and at the same time remove control of programming from the cable companies. Of course, this proposal would be anathema to those cable operators who strongly seek to enter the field of programming.

But solutions are not easily arrived at after fifty years of media growth. If television, which is the crux, is to contribute to Canadian cultural development and sovereignty, there will have to be a reorganization of the Canadian production industry and a new approach to its delivery system. The solution may not have to be so drastic or dramatic as suggested by Griffiths, but the costs and dislocation could be severe. To compete culturally with the whole world, we shall need our own production industry. It will need to be organized on a scale and in a manner to permit orderly and fair competition and geared to satisfying various audiences. A number of policy issues remain to be settled and not only in the area of jurisdiction, issues on which the artist too should be heard from. And since the long-term implications of the answers will affect generations of Canadians, it is essential that no firm decisions be made without thorough investigation of alternatives, by discussion and concrete experimentation.

The way in which a national discussion of the problems of cultural development might be carried on, given the initiative of the voluntary sector, could be along the following lines. The kind of representative group or groups mentioned earlier first approach the Secretary of State, provincial ministries of culture and others to involve them in the planning of meetings across Canada and the funding necessary to their success. At the same time the foundations and the industrial, commercial and labour communities are canvassed for funds and participation. A steering committee is formed and frames the preliminary issues, based upon analyses provided earlier by an institution, private or public, that has surveyed the views of a representative sample of the constituency most concerned. Meetings are then held in all major cities, to which all interested groups and citizens are invited and given opportunities to be heard. From these meetings the outlines of future information needs, alternative policies and methods are developed and a possible consensus arrived at; federal, provincial and municipal responsibilities are discussed, and the function of private corporations defined.

In sum, it should be possible in less than two years to hold two rounds of public meetings in at least a half dozen centres across the country.[17] With proper media coverage and an intelligent communications program to support it, the audience involved in the discussions could be varied and large. The first round of meetings would try to arrive at working definitions and principles that reflect our history and respect our constitution and traditional habits of freedom, pluralism and equity. The second round could deal with the practical application of these principles and, on the basis of the information and analyses provided and the resource people present, construct the range of policies, programs and mechanisms that would serve to connect the governmental and non-governmental bureaucracies and also link these officials and their activities to the people and objectives they are meant to serve and service. The horse-trading would have been in public where the horses' arses would be exposed along with the ways of protecting if not ridding ourselves of some of them. And the jurisdictional questions could be aired in forums that would have a practical influence on the future constitution.

More meetings, more chit-chat, it may be objected – a cop-out. But just as I suggested earlier that there is a prosy aspect to all governmental doings, there is equally a conversational, consultative, chatty aspect to all democratically arrived at decisions. This is not a time nor a country that makes consensus easy. But if we fall short of consensus, we still must understand one another's beliefs about culture. And we need a forum where it is easier than by a royal commission or task force for citizens to arrive at a *sense* of the truth about these beliefs, if not truth itself. Let the politicians, bureaucrats and artists jockey for jurisdiction openly and on the basis of the hard facts, with the emotional realities in full view. Let us find the opportunity for a sensitive Québécois to hear that being culturally unique does not have to mean being separate and that distinctive in some respects does not

201

necessarily mean superior in all respects. This is not 1750, 1850 or 1950, when assumptions of Canadian cultural dualism and "pacts" between two cultures can any longer be seriously considered by those who are not members of the elites which continue to perpetuate this tatty myth. We are all more conscious of our various heritages of cultural habits in this free country, of the differing needs we wish governments to respond to, as well as the different styles of response we expect. Inevitably, one is more conscious of the culture of the group he or she may be born into and of its status in the eyes of other Canadians than one is of other groups or of the status they perceive of themselves. What is the public reply of Easterners, for example, to the demands for equity, let alone equality, from the Western member of a minority ethnic group who knows now (like any Western WASP) that within the next two decades the descendants of "the founding peoples" will be as visibly minority cultural groups when compared with his today? Will southern Ontarians and Québécois expect to be treated as irrelevantly or as cavalierly, culturally speaking, as they have historically treated the smaller, newer groups in Western Canada? The role of insensitive elites in this process, despite the culture they may claim to represent, is nearing its end.

And if we are to have a comprehensive policy consistent with having a country, the discussion must begin soon. It will take less time and money than a royal commission and it will produce an understanding of needs that no task force, however clever, could provide. It might even produce ideas for continuing national, non-political mechanisms or commissions of stature that clever governments and bureaucrats and artists have not yet dreamed of. And where, if not at such gatherings, are we going to be able to lay bare some of the ironies and limitations that attend conflicting goals and demands? For more than fifty years every new step taken by the

202

federal government in the field of broadcasting and tele-communications has been made in the name of national identity and national unity. From Aird in the twenties through Privy Council decisions in the thirties, Voaden pressures and Turgeon Committees in the forties, Massey and Fowler reports in the fifties and sixties to the Supreme Court decisions and Bill C-24 in 1978, the litany is the same.

But what is any reasonable Canadian to make of the jungle of television blessed by government regulation, importing and repeating a majority of United States signals conveying American popular cultural products? Shades of Lecky on the impact of the telegraph in the nineteenth century! And where, if not amongst our peers, and in full view of the public, can we come to terms with those who want no government or ministerial interference in policy, but demand that certain grants be made at once to an individual project in their region?

Where else can one publicly confront the leaders of major government or voluntary organizations whom we believe have allowed their institutions to grow fat, self-satisfied and arrogant? And how else will we forge the connections that at once respect our pluralism and still develop that larger sense of community which we will need if we are to survive as a nation?

A policy or policies formed in this way would be representative and comprehensive – far and more effective for developing the free growth of Canadian culture than any political decision by any single jurisdiction.

It will be objected that the proper forum for discussion of national policy is the federal Parliament or provincial legislature. This is undeniably true. But Canadian experience with cultural policy has shown that Parliament is reluctant to discuss the question without a strong lead from the country. Certainly a full debate in Parliament should follow a program of national meetings. And the debate should be continued in party caucuses and in the parliamentary committees where cultural issues can easily be raised. And what is true for federal parliamentary participation holds equally for provincial legislatures.

The subject is one of vital interest to our continued health as a national community and to our integrity as a people. If in Canada, with all our resources of wealth and talent, we cannot work together to share our heritage of wisdom and values, our views of reality and ways of expressing them, it will be because we have missed what may well be the central meaning of our federation. For surely a confederation exists to make it possible for us to create our own life and environment. It is not just a constitutional device for taking money from the richer provinces and giving it to the poorer ones, it is not a Robin Hood organization dedicated to equalization payments and the adjustment of freight rates and seeing that the jet planes and the turbo trains run on time. Neither is it a bureaucratic device to breed larger and larger bureaucracies. It could be the potential stimulus of a living and vital culture that connects us with each other and all of us with our memories of the past and our dreams of the future.

D'Arcy McGee, the idealist of Confederation, imagined it in this light. No one is seized with patriotic feeling merely by thinking about the gross national product. It is with the eye of imagination that we perceive Canada, and perceive it as belonging to us and ourselves as belonging to it. The eye of imagination sees it as our country, our own place, our own life.

While all this is true, it must not be taken as an argument for cultural development merely to strengthen the old Confederation. To make political demands on the arts and sciences is not only self-defeating, it is dangerous. But this much can be said: without cultural development at the federal level there would be little to say for Confederation. No one need seek to justify a concern with culture from political or economic arguments. Since culture is the source of values in a society, it is its own justification. And whatever is done in politics or economics is done for and from cultural motives.

Finally, I should stress as I did in the opening chapter, that this essay is thrown out for debate. For only in democratic argument, in democratic debate, and in democratic discussion can our perceptions of cultural development be clarified and brought under scrutiny. It is time we became more conscious and rational about it and its function in all our lives. Otherwise we shall continue to be blind to the forces that shape our lives, our country and our future; and we shall fail to connect.

Apart from the changes since the Second World War, the Canada of today is still in its physical appearance and psychological outlook largely a product of the Victorian Age. The English prime minister who, with Gladstone, was to dominate that age, Victoria's favourite, Disraeli, was able to combine in his personal life the worlds of politics and culture. In the early 1840s, not long after his colleague Lord Durham had given up his struggle to find solutions to the great Canadian dilemma, Disraeli was writing the second of his famous trilogy, the novel *Coningsby*. In it, Sidonia says:

"A political institution is a machine; the motive power is the national character. With that it rests whether the machine will benefit society or destroy it. Society in this country is perplexed, almost paralyzed: in time it will move, and it will devise. How are the elements of the nation to be again blended together? In what spirit is that reorganization to take place?"

"To know that," replied Coningsby, "would be to know everything".

205

There is no remembrance of former things, neither shall there be any remembrance of things that are to come with those that shall come after.

Ecclesiastes 1:11.

The endless cycle of idea and action,
Endless invention, endless experiment,
Brings knowledge of motion, but not of stillness;
Knowledge of speech, but not of silence; . . .
Where is the Life we have lost in living?
Where is the wisdom we have lost in knowledge?
Where is the knowledge we have lost in information?

T. S. Eliot, 1934.

If one knows his neighbour's tongue, he possesses the key of his house.

Abbé Arthur Maheux, 1944.

Culture is the answer man receives when he questions nothingness.

André Malraux, 1950.

One of the signs of maturity in a culture is a sense of the need to gather and systematize information. Pioneer societies – and a pioneer society Canada largely remained until well after the end of the Second World War – are concerned with survival, and the only information that vitally interests them is practical information, the information on how things can be done. It is only when the generations pass and the inhabitants of a country become reminiscent and selfconscious, that their needs in terms of information change, and they begin to ask when and where things were done, and why.

George Woodcock, 1977.

Notes

$\mathbf{A}$lthough this little book is an essay or a tract, as one friend has called it, there may be readers or students who want to pursue the subject matter further. My views about Canadian habits, the performance of governments where culture is concerned and the centrality of culture to our lives, derive from my education and training in international, political and social history, my work experience in the voluntary, private and public sectors and a certain faith in the common sense of Canadians to solve the crises of our times.

Nevertheless, certain writers, books and articles have had direct influence on the essay itself, and most of these may be found in the notes that follow. And while it is unfortunate that no federal or provincial department or institution of government has seen fit to publish a comprehensive bibliography on the subject of culture and government, and although no university or educational organization has made available any equivalent list or analysis of what Canada and other countries have produced in this broad area of interest and study, the bibliographies appended to several of the recent works cited in the notes constitute useful alternatives.

1   Canada, Treasury Board, *Federal Expenditure Plan: How Your Tax Dollar Is Spent* (Ottawa: Minister of Supply and Services Canada, 1978), p. 59.

2   There are a number of recent examples of criticism within the community of artists and writers about the role of government in supporting cultural activities. See George Woodcock, "Democracy and the Arts of the Grecian Gifts," *Vanguard*, Aug., 1976, vol. 5, no. 6; Luke Rombout, "The Art of Politics in Canadian Arts," speech to Edmonton Art Gallery, Oct. 26, 1977; Donald B. Webster, ROM, "Canadiana: Collectors, Museums and Governments," speech to Vancouver Institute, Jan., 1976. Mordecai Richler in the Plaunt Lectures, Carleton University, 1973, touches on the relationship between government support of the arts and the mediocrity which he believes is fostered by aspects of Canadian nationalism. The various criticisms of governmental aid are by no means confined to Canada. See Eugene Ionesco: interview with *Le Figaro*, Aug. 3, 1974 (quoted in Jacques Rigaud: *La Culture pour vivre* [Paris: Gallimard, 1975]); Tom Bethell, "The Cultural Tithe," *Harper's Magazine*, Aug. 1977, pp. 18-25.

3   Organization for Economic Cooperation and Development, Reviews of National Policies for Education – Canada (Paris: 1976).

4   See T. H. B. Symons, *To Know Ourselves: The Report of the Commission on Canadian Studies*, vols. I and II (Ottawa: Association of Universities and Colleges of Canada, 1975). A summary has recently (1978) been published by McClelland and Stewart, under the title *Symons Report*. There are a few exceptions to the lack of material on both our "uncommon variety" and the lack of co-operation in presenting agreed upon facts of our

heritage, e.g. Carl F. Klinck, *Literary History of Canada: Canadian Literature in English* (Toronto: University of Toronto Press, 1976); The Canadian Ethnic Histories Series, Multicultural Program, Department of the Secretary of State, McClelland and Stewart, 1972; the series of booklets on special Canadian historical problems planned and published in both official languages by the Canadian Historical Association and distributed by the Public Archives of Canada, Ottawa; and *Dictionary of Canadian Biography* (Toronto: University of Toronto Press, 1966 –). French ed. *Dictionnaire biographique du Canada* (Québec: Presses de l'Université Laval, 1966 –); Gen. ed. F. Halpenny; Directeur adjoint: André Vachon. But the valiant efforts of organizations like the Canadian Studies Foundation made up of educationists, teachers and historians trying to fill this gap over the years has proven less successful. But the atmosphere might be changing. See Margaret Prang, "National Unity and the Uses of History," and Alfred J. Bailey, "Retrospective Thoughts of an Ethnohistorian", in *Historical Papers/ Communications Historiques*, 1977, pp. 3-12 and 15-29 resp.

5 Eli Mandel, "The Politics of Art," *The Canadian Forum*, Sept. 1977, pp. 28-29. This particular issue of the *Forum* was devoted to the subject of "Canadian Cultural Policy: A Symposium on National Pathology" and is therefore of special interest.

6 UNESCO International Fund for the Promotion of Culture, Information Document, CC/77/CONF. 003, IFPC/EXT. 2/3, Paris, Aug. 12, 1977.

7 See e.g. *The History of the Royal Hamilton Light Infantry* (Wentworth Regiment) (1862-1977), published by the RHLI Historical Association, Hamilton, 1977, in particular Chapter 7: "The Late Victorian Years." The Directorate of History of the Department of National Defence has given me access to a number of internal documents on

the history of the various cultural activities in which they
have traditionally been engaged, for which I am grateful.

8   Raymond Massey, *When I Was Young* (Toronto:
    McClelland and Stewart, 1976), p. 218.

9   D. D. Trench, Richard Chenevix, *On the Study of Words*
    (New York: The Macmillan Company, 1905), pp. 114-15.

10 Giorgio Vasari, *The Lives of the Artists* (Baltimore:
    Penguin Books, 1974), p. 30.

11 Roy Daniells, "The Cultural History of Canada –
    Centennial Project, 1982," *Royal Society of Canada,
    Proceedings & Transactions*, vol. x, 4th series, 1972, part
    2, p. 11.

12 Janet Minihan, *The Nationalization of Culture* (New
    York: New York University Press, 1977), p. 60.

13 John Vaizey, "Culture and the Cash Nexus," *Times
    Literary Supplement*, Feb. 18, 1977, p. 170. Some
    examples of various series of non-Canadian government
    publications (excluding the invaluable documentation
    from UNESCO) are: *Great Britain*: The regular
    publications of the Treasury (HMSO), the Arts Council of
    Great Britain, the Society for Education through Art, the
    Society for Theatre Research, the National Society for
    Art Education, the British Film Institute, the Museums
    Association, the Standing Commission on Museums and
    Galleries, etc. *France*: La Documentation française,
    Secrétariat d'état à la Culture, Secrétariat Général du
    Gouvernement, Direction de la Documentation, Paris
    (*Notes et études documentaires*) (Vie culturelle et pouvoirs
    publics, Paris, 1972); *Développement culturel*, bulletin
    d'information du Service des études et recherches du
    Ministère des Affaires culturelles, Paris; *Les Cahiers de la
    culture et de l'environnemenet*, Service d'information et
    de documentation, Bureau des Publications Culturelles,

Paris; *Secrétariat d'état à la Culture*: Activités, Rapport annuel, Ministère des Affaires culturelles, Paris. *United States*: The publications of the Associated Councils of the Arts; the National Research Center of the Arts; the National Committee on Cultural Resources; the American Council for the Arts in Education; the National Endowment for the Humanities; the Federal Council of the Arts and the Humanities; the Aspen Institute for Humanistic Studies. See also, *Cultural Directory: Guide to Federal Funds and Services* (New York: Associated Councils of the Arts, 1975). While Canadians like D. Paul Shafer and S. M. Crean have attempted to provide an overview of Canadian cultural development they have been handicapped by the lack and organization of Canadian data of the kind available to scholars like Janet Minihan, *op. cit.*, or Edward Skils (cf. J. Ben-David and Terry Nichols Clark, eds., *Culture and Its Creators: Essays in Honor of Edward Shils* [Chicago: University of Chicago Press, 1977]).

14 John Meisel, "Political Culture and the Politics of Culture," *Canadian Journal of Political Science*, vol. 7, no. 4, Dec. 1974, pp. 601-15.

15 Fortunately, in the past few months, there has been a renewed interest in this subject in Canada. First there was the recent announcement by the Secretary of State that Messrs. David Silcox and Yvon Desrochers will be touring the country to advise the Secretary of State on current criticisms of government programs and articulated needs of the arts community. At the same time the Conservative Party has issued a series of policy discussion papers on various aspects of cultural policy such as *New Directions in Federal Policies on Culture: The Film Industry of Canada*. Also, in Kraków, in the fall of 1977, several important scholarly papers were presented, one by Prof. John Meisel, "Leisure, Politics and Political Science: A Preliminary Exploration"; and others by Prof. Robert E. Lane, "The Regulation of

Experience: Leisure in a Market Society"; F. F. Ridley,
"State Patronage of the Arts in Britain: The Political
Culture of Cultural Politics"; and Prof. Milton C.
Cummings Jr., "To Change a Nation's Cultural Policy:
The Kennedy Administration and the Arts in the United
States, 1961-1963"; IPSA Round Table on Politics and
Culture, Kraków, 1977. These publications contribute
enormously to the subject not only as stimulating articles,
but also because of their comprehensive bibliographies.
They are to be published in *Social Science Information*,
vol. 17, no. 2, 1978. And, of course, with the publication
of the Québec White Paper on Cultural Development,
the federal government and media critics will be adding
to the discussion on an unprecedented scale.

16   J. S. Boggs, *The National Gallery of Canada* (Toronto:
     Oxford University Press, 1971), p. 17.

17   *Crestwood Heights* (Toronto: University of Toronto Press,
     1956), p. 9 ff.

18   Matthew Arnold, *Culture and Anarchy: An Essay in
     Political and Social Criticism* (London: Cambridge
     University Press, 1932).

19   Samuel Butler, "A Psalm of Montreal," *The Blasted Pine*,
     Scott & Smith ed. (Toronto: Macmillan Company, 1957),
     p. 45.

20   Percy Walker, "Questions They Never Asked Me,"
     Esquire, Dec. 1977, p. 184.

21   Edward R. Tannenbaum, *1900: The Generation Before
     the Great War* (New York: Anchor Press, Doubleday,
     1977), p. 2. "Culture gives people their view of reality. It
     includes what they know and how they know and express
     it, as well as their values and standards of behavior. Each
     culture has its own orientations to political, social and

212

economic action. And each culture has a common
structure of feeling." Tannenbaum goes on to describe
this structure of feeling in terms borrowed from David
Landes as: "a way of responding to a particular world
which in practice is not felt as one way among others – a
conscious 'way' – but is, in experience, the only way
possible." The literature attempting to define or describe
the meaning of culture is simply too extensive to try and
describe fairly in a short essay, but any reasonably
equipped library will have the titles from the classics to
the current writings clearly indexed. See also Herbert J.
Gans, *Popular Culture and High Culture* (New York:
Basic Books, 1975); Francis Jeanson, *L'Action culturelle
dans la cité* (Paris: Editions du Seuil, 1973); Maurice
Lebel, "La Culture et l'humanisme de notre âge de
transition," *Revue de l'Université d'Ottawa*, oct.-déc. 1976;
Maurice Lebel, "La Culture dans notre âge de
transition," *L'Action nationale*, fév.-mars 1977; Pierre
Aubery, "Culture prolétarienne et littérature ouvrière,"
Etudes littéraires, déc. 1974; Gilles Lane, *L'Urgence du
présent: essai sur la culture et la contre-culture* (Québec:
Presses de l'Université du Québec, 1973); and Louis
Schneider and Charles Bonjean (eds.), *The Idea of
Culture in the Social Sciences* (Cambridge, 1973).

22 Jacques Rigaud, "The Need for a Comprehensive
Cultural Policy," in *A Symposium on Culture and Society*,
reprinted from *The Great Ideas Today*, 1977 (Chicago:
Encyclopaedia Britannica, 1977), p. 34. See also the more
comprehensive development of his thesis in his book *La
Culture pour vivre* (Paris: Editions Gallimard, 1975). The
"Symposium" booklet includes an introduction by
Waldemar A. Nielsen and contributions by, in addition to
Rigaud, Arnold Goodman, Michael Straight and Philipp
Fehl, making it one of the most recent and most valuable
publications on the continuing debate. See also *Pour une
politique de la culture: au-delà des options du VIe plan*
(Paris: Editions du Seuil, 1971).

NOTES / CHAPTER TWO

1 Harold A. Innis, *The Fur Trade in Canada* (Toronto: University of Toronto Press, 1956).

2 In addition to Innis and the papers of the Hudson's Bay Company, see the works of André Vachon on this subject: André Vachon, *L'Administration de la Nouvelle-France, 1627-1760* (Toronto: University of Toronto Press; Québec: Presses de l'Université Laval, 1970), and "L'Ordre de vie dans la société indienne," (Ottawa: Canadian Historical Association, 1960). On the subject of the role of native women see Sylvia Van Kirk, "Women in Between . Indian Women in Fur Trade Society in Western Canada," *Historical Papers 1977* (Ottawa: Canadian Historical Association, 1978).

3 *The Arts in Canada* (Ottawa: Citizenship Branch, Secretary of State Department, 1967), p. 9. The existence of this school has recently been brought into question by the work of P. Moogk, "Réexamen de l'Ecole des arts et métiers de Saint-Joachim," *Revue d'histoire de l'Amérique française*, June, 1975.

4 A newspaper, *Le Canadien*, founded in 1806, was run by Etienne Parent between 1831 and 1842. François-Xavier Garneau, the leading historian of his generation, contributed to it from time to time. It was during this period that an attempt to popularize the particular ethnocentric motto of French-Canadian cultural development quoted in the text was made.

5 W. E. H. Lecky, *Democracy and Liberty* (New York: Longmans, 1896), vol. I, p. 209.

6 Harold A. Innis, *The Bias of Communication* (Toronto: University of Toronto Press, 1951; reprinted in 1964 with an introduction by Marshall McLuhan). The book

contains the lectures Innis delivered at Oxford in 1950 and was originally published by Clarendon Press, under the title *Empire and Communications*.

7 Hugh MacLennan, "The Art of City Living," *Thirty and Three* (Toronto: Macmillan Company, 1954), pp. 124-32.

8 Robert Fulford, "Notes on the Spirit of a Nation," *Saturday Night*, Special Anniversary Issue, Dec. 1977, p. 23.

9 T. H. B. Symons, *The Report on Canadian Studies*, especially vol. I., pp. 11-15.

10 Minihan, *Nationalization of Culture*, p. 40.

11 From unpublished manuscripts of Harry Bruce and Raymond Vézina on the history of the National Museums of Canada. See also Archie F. Key, *Beyond Four Walls* (Toronto: McClelland and Stewart, 1973), p. 122.

12 Minihan, op. cit., p. 89.

13 Ibid., p. 100.

14 Ibid., p. 113.

15 *The Arts in Canada*, op. cit., p. 54.

16 Boggs, *National Gallery*, p. 6; see also Bruce ms., op. cit., and National Museums Act, 1967-68, C. 21, s. 1.

17 Ian Wilson, "Shortt and Doughty: The Cultural Role of the Public Archives of Canada, 1904-1935," MA thesis, Queen's University, 1973.

18 Canada, Parliament, *House of Commons, Debates*, May 4, 1921, p. 2949.

19 Carl Berger, *The Sense of Power: Studies in the Ideas of Canadian Imperialism, 1867-1914* (Toronto: University of Toronto Press, 1970), p. 259.

20 Stephen Leacock, "Greater Canada: An Appeal," published in *University Magazine*, Apr. 1907, p. 133. This quotation in Colombo is inaccurate.

21 Marc Lescarbot is credited also with having written and produced the first Canadian play, "The Theatre of Neptune," in November 1606. For further information about libraries, see "Libraries and Archives," Statistics Canada; *"Canada Handbook, 1976"*; "Libraries in Canada," *"Encyclopedia of Library and Information Science"*, vol. 4, 1970, pp. 71-157; "Canada National Library," ibid., pp. 165-69; "Canadian Library Association," ibid., pp. 170-92. The absence of interest in cultural policy by the trade union movement of Canada and the political parties it has tried to influence from its earliest beginnings is particularly curious, given the fact that most of Canada's labour leaders have come from countries where both the trade unions and socialist movements have rarely failed to place considerable store by the cultural development of their members and indeed of the society in which they live.

22 Daniel Bell, *Cultural Contradictions of Capitalism* (New York: Basic Books, 1976), p. 11 ff.

23 T. S. Eliot, *Christianity and Culture* (New York: Harcourt, Brace and World, 1949), p. 158. "Some safeguard may be provided, against increasing centralization of control and politicization of the arts and sciences, by encouraging local initiative and responsibility, and, as far as possible, separating the central source of funds from control over their use. We shall do well also to refer to the subsidized and artificially stimulated activities each by its name; let us do what is necessary for painting and sculpture, or architecture, or

theatre, or music, or one or another science or department of intellectual exercise, speaking of each by its name and restraining ourselves from using the word 'Culture' as a comprehensive term. For thus we slip into the assumption that culture can be planned. Culture can never be wholly conscious – there is always more to it than we are conscious of; and it cannot be planned because it is also the unconscious background of all our planning."

24   In extolling the degree to which the Department of National Defence has provided assistance for cultural activities on a continuing basis for more than fifty years, I am not unaware of the references in the studies of the Royal Commission on Bilingualism and Biculturalism and in other publications and of the charges of insensitivity to the French language and French-English relations that has also been part of that department's attitude. Nonetheless, what DND systemized in the fields of historical documentation, music, performing arts, etc., cannot be dismissed by its critics simply as part of the military preoccupation with "pomp and circumstance." For further reference see: Canada, Royal Commission on Bilingualism and Biculturalism, *Report* (Ottawa: Queen's Printer, 1969), Book III, p. 329; B. Gallant, *English and French Canadians in the Armed Forces: A Historical Study* (Research report for the Royal Commission on Bilingualism and Biculturalism).

25   Rigaud, "The Need for a Comprehensive Cultural Policy," p. 34.

26   J. A. Schumpeter, *Capitalism, Socialism and Democracy* (New York: Harper and Brothers, 1950), p. 145 ff.

27   Key, *Beyond Four Walls*, p. 166; and Sir Henry Miers and S. F. Markham, *A Directory of Museums and Art Galleries; Report of a Canadian Survey* (New York: Carnegie, 1932).

28   F. W. Peers, *The Politics of Canadian Broadcasting, 1920-1951* (Toronto: University of Toronto Press, 1969).

29   Ibid., p. 44.

30   Ibid., p. 72.

31   Canadian Broadcasting Act, Chapter 24, Statutes of Canada, 1936 (Ottawa: King's Printer, 1936).

32   Martin Knelman, *This Is Where We Came In: The Career and Character of Canadian Films* (Toronto: McClelland and Stewart, 1977), p. 12 ff.

33   In January 1978, the Dominion Drama Festival was required to close down owing to lack of funds and support. See *Ottawa Journal*, Feb. 9, 1978, p. 33.

34   Canada, *Royal Commission on National Development in the Arts, Letters and Sciences, 1949-51, Report* (Ottawa King's Printer, 1951) p. 228, hereafter referred to as Massey Commission.

NOTES / CHAPTER THREE

1   Joseph Levitt, *Henri Bourassa – Catholic Critic*, Canadian Historical Association, Booklet 29 (Ottawa, 1976), p. 13. As Prof. Levitt points out, Bourassa's ideas are easily available in *Le Devoir*, 1910-1932. Levitt has provided in his pamphlet an excellent introduction to the works of both Bourassa and Groulx as follows: a selection of Bourassa's writings and speeches are to be found in J. Levitt, ed., *Henri Bourassa on Imperialism and Biculturalism, 1900-1918* (Toronto, 1970). See also Ramsay Cook, *Canada and the French-Canadian Question* (Toronto: Macmillan Company, 1966); and R. C. Brown

218

and Ramsay Cook, *Canada, 1896-1921: A Nation Transformed* (Toronto: McClelland and Stewart, 1974); A. Laurendeau, "Le Nationalisme de Bourassa," *L'Action nationale*, XLIII, Janv. 1954; L. Groulx, *Historie du Canada français depuis la découverte* (Montréal, 1953); L. Groulx, *Mes mémoires*, 2 vols. (Montréal, 1971).

2 Private papers of Herman Voaden made available to the author. See also Cummings, *op. cit.*, on the history of public financing of the arts in the United States in the thirties and forties and Ridley, *op. cit.*, for those decades in the United Kingdom.

3 Canada, Parliament, *House of Commons, Special Committee on Reconstruction and Re-establishment*, Minutes of Proceedings and Evidence (Ottawa: King's Printer, 1945). See also Voaden Papers.

4 A. R. M. Lower, "The Massey Report," *The Canadian Banker*, vol. 59, Winter 1952, pp. 22-32. See also Herschel Hardin, *A Nation Unaware* (Vancouver: J. J. Douglas Ltd., 1974), especially on the role of monopoly and the Crown corporations in Canadian economic and social history.

5 J. W. Pickersgill, *My Years with Louis St. Laurent* (Toronto: University of Toronto Press, 1975), p. 139.

6 From a taped discussion, Canadian Authors' Association, Toronto Public Library, Apr. 5, 1968, attended by Herman Voaden, John Coulter and H. Garnard Kettle.

7 Canada, Public Archives, Mackenzie King Papers, Manuscript Group 26, J1, Vol. 418, memoranda dated April 17 and April 18, 1946, pp. 37928-9.

8 J. W. Pickersgill, *op. cit.*, p. 139.

9 St. Augustine, *The City of God*, XIX-XXIV.

10   Dr. H. M. Neatby was later to write a bestseller attacking "progressive" education, *So Little for the Mind* (Toronto: Clarke Irwin, 1953).

11   Massey *Commission*, p. 3.

12   Ibid., p. 5.

13   Jean Chauvin, "Réflections sur le rapport Massey," Royal Society of Canada, *Proceedings and Transactions*, Section I, vol. 46, series 3, 1952.

14   *Winnipeg Free Press*, June 2, 1951.

15   Rigaud, "Need for a Comprehensive Cultural Policy," p. 34.

16   CBC-FM broadcast Oct. 17, 1977, Sarah Jennings, interviewer.

17   A. E. Housman, *A Shropshire Lad* (London: Richards Press, 1896), p. 92.

18   Unfortunately, a copy of this speech is not available at either the Canada Council or the Department of the Secretary of State; however, it can be seen with the permission of the Hon. J. W. Pickersgill in the St. Laurent papers at the Public Archives of Canada.

19   *Royal Commission*, 1949-51, p. 13.

20   Canada, Parliament, *House of Commons, Debates*, Feb. 6, 13, 14, 1957, pp. 1024, 1258, 1260, 1296.

21   Schumpeter, *Capitalism, Socialism and Democracy*, p. 153.

22   Lower, "The Massey Report," pp. 25, 32.

23   Bell, *Cultural Contradictions of Capitalism*, especially pp. 20, 46-54.

24 Canada Council, *Annual Report*, 1961-1962 (Ottawa: Queen's Printer, 1962).

25 Dwyer's wit is well recorded in the many annual reports whose publication he supervised. Perhaps his best-remembered story was contained in the seventh (1964) when he described the following: "When I was lunching some months ago with the Treasury Board official responsible for steering the Board to approve the expenditures of this Seminar, I asked him in my innocent way how things were progressing. He gave me that cold, beady look, characteristic of all officials concerned with the control of finances, and perhaps best described by P. G. Wodehouse as a look to be seen on the face of a parrot who is offered half a banana by a person in whose *bona fides* it does not have absolute confidence. And he said to me: "Whenever I hear the world culture . . . I reach for my purse."

NOTES / CHAPTER FOUR

1 Quoted in Marcel Rioux, *Les Québécois* (Paris: Editions du Seuil, 1974), p. 133.

2 From an interview on Radio Canada, May 5, 1952, "Revue des arts et des lettres."

3 From a speech, May 25, 1954, on receiving an honorary doctorate at St. Joseph's University (now the University of Moncton), New Brunswick.

4 *Le Devoir*, Montréal, Sept. 23, 1955.

5. According to *Colombo's Canadian Quotations* (Edmonton: Hurtig Publishers, 1974), Duplessis said: "I took you out of the gutter. Keep your mouth shut, or I'll put you back where I found you!" (p. 169).

6   Conrad Black's recent sympathetic biography of
    Duplessis, and the controversial reviews and comments it
    has evoked have stimulated new interest in Duplessis'
    career, which is reflected in part in the recent resurrection
    of the old Duplessis statue by the indepandentist
    government of René Lévesque and in a television series
    on Duplessis' career.

7   Guy Frégault, *Chronique des années perdues* (Montréal:
    Editions Lemeac, 1976), p. 157.

8   J. C. Falardeau, "Comptes rendus" (book review) on
    Chronique des années perdues Recherches sociographiques,
    vol. XVIII, no. 1, 1977, p. 159.

9   André Laurendeau, "Québec joue son rôle de capitale
    nationale du Canada français," *Le magazine Maclean*,
    Nov. 1961, 1:3.

10 Frégault, *Chronique*, p. 204.

11 Falardeau, p. 160.

12 Frégault, *Chronique*, p. 134.

13 Ibid., p. 230. See also Georges-Emile Lapalme, *Mémoires*,
    vol. 3, *Le paradis du pouvoir* (Montréal: Lemeac,1973), p.
    254.

14 Pierre Elliott Trudeau, "Les Octrois fédéraux aux
    universités," *Cité libre*, Montréal, no. 16, Fév. 1957, pp. 7-
    31.

15 George Grant, *Lament for a Nation* (Toronto:
    McClelland and Stewart, 1965). See also his *Technology
    and Empire* (Toronto: House of Anansi Press, 1969). Cf.
    S. M. Crean, *Who's Afraid of Canadian Culture?* (Don
    Mills: General Publishing Co., 1976); and James Laxer
    and Robert Laxer, *The Liberal Idea of Canada* (Toronto:
    James Lorimer and Co., 1977).

16   See the mass of evidence on this score from the data
      included in the Royal Commission on Canadian
      Economic Prospects as well as the various annual reports
      of the Economic Council of Canada and Statistics
      Canada.

17   The work of McLuhan was generously supported by the
      Ford Foundation, and in 1963 he was given a Governor
      General's Award for his book *The Gutenberg Galaxy.*

18   Pelletier to the author, June 18, 1977.

19   Under Juneau's leadership, the work of the Commission
      gradually fused regulation with policy making to a degree
      that eventually led the government to believe that the
      Commission was exceeding its authority. This conviction
      was in part responsible for the Government decision to
      table Bill C-43, later amended to C-24 in 1978 which
      formally established the authority of the Minister of
      Communications to vary the decisions of the Canadian
      Radio-Television Commission and to become the single
      ministerial focus for Canadian broadcasting policy.

20   *Report of the Royal Commission on Bilingualism and
      Biculturalism,* vol. 1-5 (Ottawa, Oct. 1967-Feb. 1970);
      Charter of the French Language, Statutes of Quebec,
      Chapter 5, Aug. 26, 1977 (Bill 101); *A Science Policy
      for Canada: Report of the Senate Special Committee on
      Science Policy,* Hon. Maurice Lamontagne, Chairman
      (Ottawa: Senate of Canada, 1970). The federal
      government has been involved in scientific activities,
      given the history of exploration and exploitation of our
      national resources, since Confederation. The National
      Research Council was founded in 1917 as the principal
      federal agency to encourage research in all the sciences
      but particularly in those that could best influence the
      development of industry. Today, of course, with a budget
      approaching the quarter of a billion dollar level, its
      interests are much broader and its impact on the
      directions of scientific development are enormously

important to all Canadians. In 1966, the government established the Science Council of Canada to assess independently our science and technology resource needs and potential and the Council's many useful studies have had a significant impact on federal agencies as well as universities. But all this effort and infrastructure is today threatened by the decisions to cut back the pace of investment in such pursuits and the terrible erosion of financial resources by inflation is crippling the progress that has been achieved to date.

21 CBC interview, Feb. 2, 1965.

NOTES / CHAPTER FIVE

1 See examples of this philosophy and policy in the range of official Liberal Party literature of the campaign and general press coverage, notably: Liberal Party of Canada, *Liberal Party Policy Statement* (Ottawa, 1968); Liberal Federation of Canada, *Pierre Elliott Trudeau: Today and Tomorrow* (Ottawa, n.d.); Claude Hénault, "Equal Status for New Canadians: Trudeau Explains His 'Just Society!'," Toronto *Telegram*, Oct. 28, 1968; "What Made Trudeau Decide to Run," *Globe and Mail*, Feb. 17, 1968. The recommendations of the Prime Minister's Task Force on government information exemplify the mood and policies of the times.

2 The policy of democratization and decentralization (outlined by Pelletier in two early speeches, one in Lethbridge, Mar. 10, 1969, and the other in Venice, Aug. 27, 1970) was pursued by the National Museums of Canada not only at the request of the Secretary of State, the Hon. J. Hugh Faulkner, but also because the Board of the National Museums was strongly supportive of the philosophy and of the need to establish programs that

224

reflected it, if the Museums were to become truly national. The role of the Department of the Secretary of State had been questioned in earlier years by officials at the PCO whose task it is to review general government operations and structures. But the determination of the government after 1972 to refuse support to programs related to the philosophy of participatory democracy, the transformation of OFY from a responsive, socially-oriented youth program into an employment program run by the Manpower Department, the hiving-off of the multiculturalism programs to a minister not associated with the Secretary of State Department, and the increasing criticism of the Translation and Bilingualism Divisions within and outside the government, inevitably raised the question of the future of the Department again.

3 Cultural Property Export and Import Act, *Statutes of Canada, 1974-75-76*, Chapter 50 (Ottawa: Queen's Printer, 1976).

4 One reason that politicians are not impressed arises from the confusion about such data created by economists trying to wrestle with the problem. See the most recent example of this conflict of opinion in the panel discussion during the annual meeting of the Canadian Conference of the Arts in Halifax on April 27, 1978, where Eric Kierans, Brian Dixon, Marie-Josée Drouin, John Godfrey and Alvin Reiss could agree on almst nothing.

5 Carol Kirsh, *A Leisure Study* (Ottawa: Secretary of State Department, 1972). In 1975, a further study was done but, unfortunately, as the report points out on page 32, No. 2.7ff, " ... comparisons between the participation rates and levels of involvement recorded by the 1975 Survey are somewhat difficult to make."

6 Robert Martin, "Canada's Film Industry Comes of Age – At Last," *Globe and Mail*, Nov. 19, 1977, p. 35.

7   Canada, Dept. of the Secretary of State, *The Film Industry in Canada* (Ottawa: 1976).

8   Communiqué issued by the Hon. Jean Chrétien, Minister of Indian Affairs and Northern Development, Sept. 12, 1972. The formal constitution under which Heritage Canada operates is available from its headquarters in Ottawa.

NOTES / CHAPTER SIX

1   Raymond Morrissette entered the Minister's cabinet when Jean-Noël Tremblay was appointed in 1966; he became assistant deputy minister in 1967 and replaced Mr. Frégault in 1968. He is now adviser to the Québec delegation in Paris.

2   Québec (Province). *Commission d'enquête sur l'enseignement des arts au Québec, Rapport* (Québec: Editeur officiel, 1969).

3   "Le Rapport du tribunal de la culture," *Liberté*, Déc. 1976. Cf. Nicole Boily and François Marc Gagnon, "L'Enracinement de l'art du Québec – problématiques des années 1920-1945," *Critère*, janv. 1974; Jean Eudes Landry, "Culture – le verdict et l'appel," *Loisirs plus*, fév. 1976; A. Paradis, "Feu vert à la culture: éditorial," *Vie des arts*, automne 1976; Jean-Noël Tremblay, "Les Combats parallèles," *Revue de l'Association canadienne d'éducation de langue française*, avr. 1976. Cf., Marcel Rioux, "Communities and Identity in Canada," *Options* (Toronto, Oct. 1977).

4   See William Johnson's article criticizing David Thomas's allegations as "unsubstantiated" in *Globe and Mail*, March 4, 1978, p. 13. See also other newspaper responses

to later leaks: "PQ Plans to Dispense Basic Culture,"
Globe and Mail, May 8, 1978; Québec to Regulate
Operations of Media," ibid.; "White Paper Is Nothing to
Fear: Laurin," *Montreal Gazette*, May 8, 1978: "Contrôle
plus serré des moyens de communication," *La Presse*,
May 8, 1978; "Controlling the Québec Media," *Ottawa
Citizen*, May 9, 1978; "La Difficile gestation d'un livre
blanc," *Le Devoir*, May 10, 1978. By July, the P.Q.
through Louis O'Neill was already indicating a reluctance
to proceed with its press agency ideas, *The Gazette*,
Montreal, July 14, 1978.

5   *La Politique québécoise du développement culturel*, 2 vols.
Le ministre d'Etat au Développement culturel (Québec:
Editeur officiel, 1978).

6   Toronto's cultural support is double-tiered: Metro
(regional) and City of Toronto (one of the six constituent
boroughs). The 1978 budgets are: Metro Toronto: Grants
– $1,750,000; O'Keefe Centre – $1,261,900; Total:
$3,011,900. City of Toronto: Grants–$440,000; St.
Lawrence Centre – $334,760; Total: $774,760. Both totals
adding an approximate amount for salaries which are
hidden in other budgets, would amount to a budget of
over $4 million. It has been suggested that the other five
boroughs (North York, Scarborough, Etobicoke, York
and East York) contribute up to $100,000 amongst them.

7   E.g., *Eléments pour une politique culturelle en Suisse*:
Rapport de la Commission fédérale d'experts pour
l'étude de questions concernant la politique culturelle
suisse, Berne, 1975; *New Cultural Policy in Sweden*,
Swedish National Council for Cultural Affairs and the
Swedish Institute, Stockholm, 1973; *Support for the Arts
in England and Wales*, Lord Redcliffe-Maud, Calouste
Gulbenkian Foundation, London, 1976. Since Malraux's
administration, in the sixties, of the French Ministry of
Culture it has been engaged in a continuous policy
review and the latest restructuring and financing can be

found in the legislation tabled before the National
Assembly in the past year. Since the Kennedy
Administration of the early 60s there have been
continuous examinations of financial support of the arts
in the U.S. by the White House staff, federal and
federally supported agencies. The most recent have been
referred to in the text and "notes", especially the work of
Michael Straight and his assistants. See also Cummings,
op. cit.

8   In 1962 I was firmly of the belief, as is recorded in my
    book *Research in the Humanities and in the Social
    Sciences of Canada* (Ottawa: Humanities Research
    Council of Canada and the Social Science Research
    Council of Canada, 1962), that dividing the Council
    would ensure greater parliamentary financial support for
    the humanities and social sciences on the one hand, and
    the performing arts on the other. This was a period when
    the Canada Council's budget was at its lowest and when
    the needs of the universities in support of graduate
    students and the research libraries to assist them was at
    its peak. I believed then that by dividing the two, the
    lobbyists for each would be able to attract far more
    attention from the bureaucracy and Parliament and
    extract the resources each division needed. At the time
    even Mr. Lamontagne was a supporter of this view. But
    the increase of funding for the Canada Council changed
    the need to separate the disciplines and indeed, today it is
    extraordinarily hard to follow the logic which has led to
    the split.

NOTES / CHAPTER SEVEN

1   Morley Callaghan, "The Morality of Security: the Politics
    of Privacy," *Toronto Life*, Jan. 1978, p. 94. Cf. Robin
    Mathews, *Canadian Literature: Surrender or Revolt*
    (Toronto: Steel Rail Press, 1978).

2   In October 1977, UNESCO sponsored a meeting in Paris
    where representatives of ten countries, including Canada,
    discussed "the international standardization of statistics
    of public expenditure on cultural activities." The meeting
    was chaired by the Canadian representative, Yvon
    Ferland of Statistics Canada, and received three major
    studies: "Methodological Study on Public Expenditure
    for Culture," by Tapio Kanninen and Eskos Roos of the
    Finnish Central Statistical Office; "Analysis of Public
    Expenditure on Culture," by Auguste Vesse, INSEE,
    France; and "Statistics on Public Expenditure for
    Culture," by Gabor Koncz, Institute for Culture,
    Budapest. Considerable progress was made on definitions
    and technical issues and while there was little hesitation
    in admitting to some of the grave problems confronting
    the main question, it was agreed to continue and build
    upon this important exchange of ideas. (ADS-77/STC-7/
    CONF.602/COL6). See also "Community Action in the
    Cultural Sector," *Bulletin of the European Communities*,
    Supplement 6/77, Belgium, and "Stats Can Moves in on
    Culture," *The Citizen*, May 18, 1978, p. 89.

3   Alvin Toffler, "The Art of Measuring the Arts,"
    American Academy of Political and Social Science,
    Annals, Philadelphia, Sept. 1967. In addition, see
    "Toward a Social Report," U.S. Government Printing
    Office, Washington, D.C. and the critical analysis of it in
    The Public Interest, No. 15, Spring 1969, pp. 72-117,
    published by National Affairs Inc., New York and
    Raymond A. Bauer (ed.), *Social Indicators* (Cambridge:
    the M.I.T. Press, 1967). Also, readers might be interested
    in a short Canadian article published in *Canadian Public
    Policy/Analyse de Politiques*, vol. II, no. 1, Winter 1976,
    by Steven Globerman and Sam H. Book, entitled
    "Formulating Cost and Output Policies in the Performing
    Arts".

4   G. Bruce Doern, "Recent Changes in the Philosophy of
    Policy Making in Canada," *Canadian Journal of Political
    Science*, June 1971, p. 269.

5   The Canadian government tax system, in spite of the
    principle of equity which its authors maintain is the basis
    of the law, has always found justification for supporting
    special needs or special groups of Canadians in the
    national interest. The most recent example is in the
    budget of April 1978, when special tax benefits were
    made available to the business community for scientific
    research in the interest of industrial development. An
    even stronger case could be made for providing a 150 per
    cent tax write-off in the interest of acquiring from abroad
    the few remaining great works of art and artifacts for the
    museums and galleries of this country. We are already
    benefiting from the important tax changes to assist film
    ventures.

6   The present formula, in effect till December 1979, for the
    annual distribution of the net profits of the annual draws
    of Loto Canada is as follows: 82½ per cent to reimburse
    the Province of Québec for its debt associated with the
    Olympic Games and for the debt assumed for the
    Commonwealth Games in Edmonton; 12½ per cent to
    each province based on the number of tickets sold in that
    province, each province including Québec receiving their
    proportion of the total; the balance of 5 per cent going to
    Fitness and Amateur Sports at the Department of Health
    and Welfare. By December 1979, most of the moneys to
    cover the Olympic debt will have been paid out, and
    therefore, the commitment of this federal funding beyond
    1979 becomes of immense importance, especially for
    those programs that are clearly non-partisan and of social
    benefit, such as cultural ones. A reasonable distribution
    might be to continue a distribution to the provinces based
    on sales of 50 per cent, raise the 5 per cent going to sport
    and fitness to 25 per cent of the balance and reserve 25
    per cent for culture and related projects. On the basis of
    current net profit of Loto Canada, this would provide a
    substantial increase for federal cultural programs without
    in any way affecting the tax payer except, perhaps, to

230

reduce what he might eventually have to pay to assist Canadian or provincial cultural projects.

7   John A. Porter, *The Vertical Mosaic: An Analysis of Social Class and Power in Canada* (Toronto: University of Toronto Press, 1968).

8   The Rt. Hon. Kenneth Robinson, "Support for the Arts – The Next Five Years," Alport Lecture, City University, London, England, June 16, 1977.

9   Kildare Dobbs, literary editor for the *Toronto Star*, 1973.

10 The Hon. Gérard Pelletier, from a speech made to the Intergovernmental Conference on Institutional, Administrative and Financial Aspects of Cultural Policies, Venice, Aug. 27, 1970. At that time, Pelletier was Secretary of State of Canada and leader of the Canadian delegation to the above conference. The Hon. John Roberts addressed a similar theme at the annual meeting of the Canadian Conference of the Arts in Halifax, Apr. 28, 1978.

11 Robert Welch, "Government Involvement in the Arts Offers a Dangerous Dilemma," *The Arts in Canada: Today and tomorrow*, Report on the 45th Couchiching Conference of the Canadian Institute of Public Affairs, 1976.

12 See footnote 2, Chapter One.

13 Economic Council of Canada, *Eighth Annual Review: "Design for Decision-Making – An Application to Human Resources Policies"* (Ottawa, 1971), p. 80.

14 *Arts in Canada*, p. 153. A. R. Megarry, "The Information Society," Presentation to the Science Council of Canada, Feb. 9, 1978; D. F. Parkhill, "The Future of Computer

Communications," *CIPS Session '78*, Canadian
Computer Conference, Edmonton, May 1978; Canadian
Radio-Television and Telecommunications Commission,
Report on Pay-Television (Ottawa: CRTC, 1978).

15   The question of cable's status is dealt with in a
forthcoming background study by Robert E. Babe,
*Canadian Television Broadcasting, Structure: Performance
and Regulation*, to be published by the Economic Council
of Canada. The question was also discussed by the
Minister of Communications in a speech to the Canadian
Cable Television Association, May 1978, and at a seminar
on the Conserver Society by the chairman of the federal
Advisory Board on Communications Research, Mr. J.
Alphonse Ouimet, *Globe and Mail*, Apr. 25, 1978, p. B5.

16   Stuart Griffiths, "Alternatives for Canadian Television,"
Commission Study Submitted to the Ontario Royal
Commission on Violence in the Communications
Industry, 1977.

17   See footnote 4, Chapter Six. In the case of Sweden, it took
ten years to produce the report and two years for their
national legislature to pass the major recommendations in
it. This may sound a little excessive, but most of the other
major reports have taken several years to produce and
several more to carry out their proposals, so that the
time-frame suggested for this "peoples" royal commission
could prove relatively short.

INDEX

Hamilton Art Gallery (1912), 37
Harris, Lawren, 44
Hearne, Samuel, 18
Hébert, Louis-Philippe, 39
Herbert, Walter, 70
Heritage Canada, 133
Howe, C.D., 46, 66
Howe, Joseph, 36
Hudson's Bay Company, 17, 18, 23 36
Humanities Association of Canada, 70
Humanities Research Council, 70
Huot, Charles-Edouard, 39

Identity, culture and, 3, 5, 6, 7, 18, 27
Immigrants, traditions brought, 25-6,
  28; early attitudes towards, 26, 28; in
  Quebec, 94
Imperial Order of Daughters of the
  Empire (1900), 40
Innis, Harold, 17, 19
Institut Canadien, 36
L'Institut canadien des affaires
  publiques, conference (1955), 82
L'Institut national de la civilisation, 145
L'Institut québécois du cinéma, 152-3

Jameson, Anna, 16
Jesuits, 36
Jobin, Louis, 39
Jobin, Raoul, 75, 88
Johnson, Daniel, 144
Julien, Henri, 39
Juneau, Pierre, 104

Keynes, John Maynard, Baron Keynes,
  54, 192
Killam, Isaak Walton, 67
King, William Lyon Mackenzie, 57-8,
  112
Knelman, Martin, 47

Lagerlöf, Selma, 112
L'Allier, Jean-Paul, 150, 153; Green
  Paper, 153-6
La Marsh, Judy, 101, 106
Lamontagne, Maurice, 67, 79, 100-101,
  104
Lampman, Archibald, 50
Lapalme, Georges-Emile, 88, 92, 94
Laporte, Pierre, 94, 142
Laurendeau, André, 89; B&B
  Commission, 106-7

Laurier, Sir Wilfrid, 16, 32-3, 50, 78,
  140
Laurin, Camille, 157, 160, 162
Laval, François de, 21
Leacock, Stephen, 35
Leblond, Jacques, 21
Lecky, W. E. H., 24
Leduc, Ozias, 39
Léger, Jules, 117-9, 174
Le Pan, Douglas, 53, 74
Lesage, Jean, 86, 88
Lescarbot, Marc, 36
Lévesque, Georges-Henri, 60, 63, 66,
  74-5, 81-3
Lévesque, René, 82, 86, 147
Lévi-Strauss, Claude, 20
Libraries, public, 35-6, 73; National
  Library Act, 102
Literary and Historical Society of
  Québec, 30, 36
Local Initiatives Program (LIP), 119
Lorne, J. D. S. Campbell, Marquess of,
  32
Louis XIV, 20
Louvre, 30
Low, Solon, 71
Lower, A. R. M., 55-6, 73
Luc, Frère, 21
Lussier, Charles, 90
Lyman, John, 53

Macdonald, Sir John A., 50, 174
McClelland and Stewart, 121

McGee, Thomas D'Arcy, 14, 33, 50, 204
MacKenzie, Dr. Norman A. M., 61
MacLennan, Hugh, 26, 75
McLuhan, Marshall, 116
MacMillan, Sir Ernest, 54, 56
Macphail, Agnes, 50
Malraux, André, 90, 96, 115, 206
Mandel, Eli, 4
Manitoba, early cultural institutions,
  37; present cultural departments, 137;
  culture and recreation expenditures,
  136-7
Manitoba Music Festival, 37
Manitoba Schools Act, 22
Manitoba Society of Artists, 37
"March on Ottawa" (1944), 54
Marchand, Jean, 147

238

Royal Commission on Status of
Women, 118
Royal Commission on Violence in
Broadcasting (Ontario), 199
Royal Ontario Museum, 38
Royal Society of Canada, 70
Ryan, Claude, 193
Ryerson, Egerton, 36

Saint-Exupéry, A. de, 50
St. Laurent, Louis, 58, 60, 66-9, 99
St-Sulpice library, 88
Saskatchewan, provincial cultural
departments, 137; culture and
recreation expenditures, 135-7
Saturday Night, 26
Sauvé, Paul, 86
Savard, Félix-Antoine, 163-4
Schumpeter, Joseph A., 42, 72
Scott, F. R., 75
Sculptors' Society of Canada, 47, 54
Sculpture, wood, 21, 39
Secretary of State, Department of,
transfer of cultural agencies to, 100;
early activities 101-2; responsibilities
re agencies, 105; procedural changes,
106; cultural activities, 114-6, 117-9,
120-1; structure, 117; funding, 123,
127, 131-34; present responsibilities,
130; *see* Federal cultural policy
Separatism, 80-82, 162-4; *see*
Nationalism
Service du Canada français d'outre-
frontières, 90
Shadbolt, Jack, 75
Shakespeare Society, 37
Shirley, James, 13
Shortt, Adam, 34
Simpson, Sir George, 18
Smith, A. J. M., 75
Smith, Goldwyn, 38
Smith, Norman, 45
Smithsonian Institution, 30
Social Science Research Council, 70
Sociéte des écrivains canadiens, 47, 54,
56
Société des éditeurs canadiens, 92
Société des éditeurs de manuels
scolaires, 92
Société historique de Montréal, 36
Société des librairies, 92
Société Saint-Jean-Baptiste, 40

Society of Arts (U.K.), 31
Special Committee on Reconstruction
and Re-establishment, *see* Turgeon
Committee
Special Senate Committee on Science
Policy (1967), 109
Spry, Graham, 45
Standing Committee on Broadcasting,
Film and Assistance to the Arts (1965),
105
Statistics Canada, 184
Stratford Shakespearian Festival, 76
Surveyer, Arthur, 60, 65

Taché, Eugène, 174
The Tamarack Review, 76
Tawney, R.H., 179
Technology, exchange through fur
trade, 17, 18, 19; cultural effects, 23-4,
27; effects of automation, 74,
unemployment, 119; *see* Cable
television
Telegraph, cultural effects, 23-5
Television, 61; *see* CBC, Cable television
Theatre, Québec, 92-3; *see* Performing
arts
Le Théatre du Nouveau Monde, 76
Thériault, Yves, 75
Thornton, Sir Henry, 44, 60, 66
Time, 121
Tonnancour, Jacques de, 53
Toronto, cultural funding, 165, 226
Tremblay, Jean-Noël, 144-7
Trench, Richard Chenevix, 5
Troika Committee, on broadcasting,
103
Trudeau, Pierre Elliott, 95, 105, 147
Turgeon Committee (1944), on arts in
Canada, 54-7

UNESCO, International Fund for the
Promotion of Culture, 4-5; Canadian
delegation (1946), 56; Canadian
National Commission, 132
United States of America, 7, 30, 43,
124; *see* Americanization

Valcourt, Jean, 88
Valéry, Paul, 140
Vancouver Little Theatre Association,
37
Vancouver Symphony Society, 37